THE EXTRAORDINARY ORDINARY PRISONER

ESSAYS FROM INSIDE AMERICA'S CARCERAL STATE

JEREMIAH BOURGEOIS

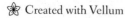

CONTENTS

FOREWORD

Stephen Handelman
Editor, *The Crime Report*

On June 7, 2016, an email appeared in our inbox from someone offering to write for *The Crime Report*. We've received many similar inquiries over the years, but the last line in the message caught our attention. "I realize that submissions should include more information," the writer said. "However, I hope you overlook that requirement in light of the fact that I am incarcerated."

The author of the message identified himself as Jeremiah Bourgeois, Prisoner #708897, then confined to the Stafford Creek Corrections Center, a mixed medium-minimum security prison for men located five miles from Aberdeen, Washington, on the Pacific coast. As we learned later, Jeremiah's communications from prison had to travel a circuitous route, relayed through his fiancée, Aimée Muul, in Seattle.

"Prison writing" is a genre of its own. Writers such as André Gide, Eldridge Cleaver, Bobby Sands, and Arthur Longworth have used their confinement as an opportunity for political protest, as a reckoning with the world they left behind, or simply as a way to pursue self-knowledge. PEN, the international writers' organization, has its own section devoted entirely to writers who are, or have been, behind bars. The Crime Report has regularly published writing of youths in juvenile detention and other facilities nurtured by the Beat Within project in San Francisco.

Jeremiah Bourgeois turned out to be special for a number of reasons.

When he wrote us, he was 38 years old—and had already spent the previous 24 years behind bars for the May 19, 1992, revenge killing of Seattle store owner Tecle Ghebremichale, who had testified against his brother in an assault case. Aged 14 at the time of his crime, he was sentenced to life without parole. It was the era before the Supreme Court ruled such sentences for juveniles unconstitutional, and Jeremiah had every reason to expect he would spend the rest of his life in prison. "It was probably the saddest case I've ever had," his lawyer, Michael Trickey, told the *Seattle Times* in 2005, noting both Jeremiah's age and length of sentence.

Jeremiah spent much of his first decade in prison in a permanent state of anger and defensiveness, frequently in conflict with corrections officers and fellow inmates. But then something changed. Prisoner #708897, as he would later write, realized that he was on a path to self-destruction. He began reinventing and reeducating himself through long hours in the prison library. That's not unusual—prison libraries, even though many are poorly stocked, have been the salvation of countless inmates. Jeremiah's emergence as an independent, often contrarian, voice was especially timely in a debate about mass incarceration that has often gotten bogged down in rhetoric.

By the time he came to us, he had already become a blogger on *Minutes Before Six* and had published research articles for scholarly journals. As an occasional, and then a regular, columnist for *The Crime Report*, Jeremiah honed his considerable talents to shape a writing personality that resonated with readers across the country, judging by the comments posted on our website (including some who were also incarcerated). His 36 columns over the past three years, on subjects such as the treatment of gay and transgender prisoners, the lack of a #MeToo movement for incarcerated women, and the hypocrisies of prison "family visitation" events, were at times bitter, but invariably thought-provoking. They measured the distance between the idealism of advocates "outside" and the bleak realities of day-to-day life inside.

On October 28, 2019, after multiple unsuccessful attempts to gain parole, he finally was released from captivity—only to begin an even more difficult process of adjustment to a world he had not seen for more than a quarter century.

We're honored that Jeremiah will continue to chronicle the next steps of that journey for The Crime Report. Meanwhile, this edited collection of 17 columns written from prison—and one when he finally got out—is an introduction to the remarkable personal odyssey of what he described, in another context, as an "extraordinary ordinary prisoner."

For those of you who have been following his writing since 2016, it will be a welcome opportunity to re-engage with a unique writer. Those reading him for the first time will find inspiration. And for all of us, Jeremiah's prison writing is evidence that it's possible to find redemption and rehabilitation even at the heart of the carceral state.

For ex-Prisoner #708897, real life is beginning again. But it remains important to remember that there are two million Americans still locked behind cell bars, including more than 2,300 inmates sentenced to spend the rest of their lives imprisoned for violent crimes committed when they were juveniles like Jeremiah. Their lives are still on hold.

BREAKING GOOD: HOW TO HEAL A LIFE SPENT BEHIND BARS

On Aug, 15, 2017, in his 25th year of captivity, Jeremiah Bourgeois had his first parole hearing, thanks to legislative changes made in response to a Supreme Court ruling in 2012 that rendered his sentence unconstitutional.[1] It was to be the first of several abortive attempts at gaining his freedom, but in one of his early columns for The Crime Report, he was already thinking of what it meant to "deserve" a second chance after a terrible crime.

Two weeks ago, on August 15, 2017, I had my first parole hearing.

I have been confined since 1992. At the age of 14, I murdered a convenience-store owner and wounded his business partner after one of the men finished testifying against my then-15-year-old brother. Several months earlier, my brother had shot the man I later killed, along with another of the store's co-owners.

In the 25 years since, I've obtained a college education, I have written in academic journals, and I am now a regular columnist for *The Crime Report*. I intend to earn my master's degree if the parole board sets me free. My brother (who spent four years in a juvenile detention facility for his crimes) is now a mortgage broker, a home-owner, a devoted father, and a little league coach.

Our lives illustrate that prisoners do not have to be defined by the commission of (even heinous) crimes.

As for the victims, there is no happy ending.

Those who survived the shootings were forced to abandon their convenience store. The American Dream that they pursued after immigrating to this country from war-torn Eritrea was gone. While I was engaged in college studies, the murder victim's family decided to return to East Africa rather than remain in America's inner city.

Their lives powerfully illustrate victimization.

No matter my remorse and personal reform, I cannot undo this tragedy. This truth often brings the following question to my mind: What do I owe society in the event that I am freed?

I rarely hear this question posed behind prison walls.

I have watched countless men serve lengthy sentences, and the prevailing sentiment is that their imprisonment satisfies the "debt" owed to society. They believe that one's loss of liberty serves to wipe the slate clean.

Typically, the most positive thing that I hear men express as their release dates approach is a commitment to be a "square" and make a living by working legitimately.

They pledge to forsake friends who are still "in the game," and vow they'll no longer abuse drugs—or rather, to only smoke mari-juana occasionally.

They desire to have a relationship with a "solid female" and want to raise a family.

All of this is a perfectly fine strategy for not becoming a recidivist. But why should crime desistance be the sole measure of rehabilita-tion and successful reintegration?

Why do so many prisoners give little heed to the notion of restoration?

It is true that making amends to the victims of violent crimes is—all too often—impossible to achieve. Still, there are countless ways in which we can try to improve the communities where we caused so much pain and suffering.

Last year at Stafford Creek Corrections Center, Matthew Emerzian, the founder of a California-based not-for-profit group called "Every Monday Matters,"[2] illuminated ways that people can make positive changes in their community. He has carried his message of achieving positive change by setting goals every Monday of the year ("52 Mondays") across the country to get citizens involved in his cause.

But this was the first time he had relayed it to a group of people locked away in a penitentiary.

After receiving a poignant letter from a prisoner at Stafford Creek, Emerzian pulled the necessary strings to give a presentation about his life and his program to approximately 100 men seated attentively in the visiting room.

I was among them.

On that day, we learned that the mission of Every Monday Matters is to get people to take "personal responsibility to make a difference. To matter—one day, one action at a time, " Emerzian explained.

He also summarized the 2007 book he co-authored with Kelly Bozza, which highlights "the benefits of your actions and the collective actions of many" and provides "a specific plan for exactly what you can do and where you can go to make a difference. "[3]

Emerzian had never been imprisoned. Still, his personal narrative on how his wealth and success could not inoculate him against depression, and that his efforts to make a difference brought new meaning to his life, was compelling.

However, I must admit that I felt his message was empty rhetoric in the confines of a prison environment. In my experience, prisoners who seek to change *this* community find themselves transformed for the worse. They become consumed by frustration and despair.

As I sat quietly in the room, I began to feel unease when I saw the enraptured looks on the faces of the prison administrators who were listening.

I saw how easy this program could be hijacked—if Emerzian was seduced by the DOC—and morph into something purported to be reformative but devoid of transformational qualities.

This is no conspiracy theory.

Behind the pretense of rehabilitation, the object of prison is retribution and incapacitation, both of which are accomplished through coercion and compulsion. I wasn't the only one who was skeptical. As one commentator on the restorative justice concept noted,[4] there are reasons to doubt whether a "constructive ethos" can be integrated "within a punishment-based social institution such as a prison."

Such projects are often a foil "used to add legitimacy to an institution which remains essentially punitive," according to Odillo Vidoni Guidoni, who was involved in creating a restorative justice program at a prison in Italy.[5]

With such thoughts running through my mind as I listened to Emerzian and bore witness to administrative glee, I decided to tune out the subsequent brainstorm session on ways to transform Stafford Creek into a community where, hereto, "Every Monday Matters." The entire notion seemed pretentious and ridiculous.

I was having none of it.

A year later, Emerzian's creed has come back to me and I now see the importance of his message.

My change of heart was prompted when a member of the parole board asked me during my hearing, "If you could say anything to the son of the man that you killed, what would you tell him?"

The question shook me.

I doubt that I will ever forget the feelings of self-loathing and grief that flooded me as I answered the question.

These are the emotions that I have tried mightily to subsume despite my remorse for my crimes.

As these feelings overwhelmed me, I came to see why prisoners readily accept the proposition that one's loss of liberty sets things right, for embracing this fiction is nepenthe to relieve the troubled psyche.

Pragmatically, I agree that it seems sensible for prisoners on the verge of release to focus their attention on how to get back on their feet, rather than bettering their community given the impediments to reentry.

But staying free and making a difference are not mutually exclusive.

Nor is devoting oneself to being a "square" from here forward the sole prescription for avoiding recidivism.

It may not be a novel concept, but I have come to believe that developing a social conscience can go a long way towards reducing the risk of re-offending. In fact, putting it into practice is not as difficult as it may seem.

Emerzian and Bozza highlight "52 Mondays to make a difference" by doing things as simple as donating blood, planting a tree, or treating the homeless with dignity. Some might think this is corny, but it's a useful way to avoid the mindset that leads two out of three former prisoners to return to the penitentiary.[6]

When one endeavors to do something positive for society it inculcates morality. In so doing, a former prisoner's likelihood of reoffending diminishes because he or she sees the value of being a benefit to his community.

At least that's my theory. I hope to one day practice what I'm preaching.

The parole board will determine my destiny by September 15, 2017. If given the opportunity to be freed, I will indeed make Every Monday Matter.

It is the least I can do for society.

For my humanity.

I have left many victims in my wake. As have countless others behind bars. We all have a moral imperative to try to forge justice from the injustices we commit.

A weekly activity aimed at making "a difference in a small but significant way" can accomplish more than Emerzian originally conceived. For someone like me, it is one of the few ways to make amends for all my wrongdoing.

—*Aug. 29, 2017*

2

'I DON'T KNOW IF I WILL EVER BE ABLE TO GET OVER THIS'

That parole hearing did not go well. In the face of crushing disappointment, Jeremiah appeared to be losing hope.

Across the United States, there are hundreds of prisoners serving sentences of life without the possibility of parole for crimes committed when they were juveniles, but who now have an opportunity to be freed from newly imposed indeterminate sentences once they complete lengthy minimum terms of confinement.

I am one of them.

Call us the "Miller family"—after the 2012 Supreme Court *Miller vs. Alabama*[1] ruling that determined imposing a life-without-parole sentence on a juvenile convicted of murder violated constitutional protections from cruel and unusual punishment.

My original sentence was imposed for crimes that I committed when I was 14. However, in light of the Court's ruling, the Washington State legislature gave prisoners like me the opportunity to be freed—provided that we are deemed by the parole board to be unlikely to "commit new criminal law violations if released."

I must admit I rejoiced at this news. I had by then served 20 years of a natural-life sentence. Yet as I moved closer to completing my newly imposed minimum term, I came to realize that the light at the end of the tunnel might actually be a train.

I had watched my former cellmate, Anthony Powers, lose his petition for parole even though, in the view of many who knew him, including the then-Deputy Secretary of the Washington Department of Corrections (WDOC), he was a model of reform.

That official wrote to Powers declaring that he recognized "*his contributions to making Washington State prisons safer for both offenders and staff.*"

"*Your efforts,*" he continued, "*have made a difference. I also believe those efforts will continue to make a difference for the men that are released back into the community ... I encourage you to continue to be a role model for other offenders. You have made a difference in many lives.*"

Nevertheless, when Powers later underwent the requisite psychological assessment to determine whether he posed a recidivism risk, the conclusion was that he posed a high risk to reoffend.

This made me wary—for the arc of our lives had striking similarities. I too had committed a heinous crime when I was a teen.[2] Therefore, to my mind, if it could be said that "a role model for other offenders" posed a risk to public safety, surely the same could be said for me.

My history provided all the elements necessary to craft a narrative to support either keeping me confined permanently—or setting me free—notwithstanding the results of a potentially negative psychological risk analysis.

The case for freedom could summarize, as I wrote in an earlier column for *The Crime Report,* that "I used to be dangerous. Now I can effectively speak in public. I can present cogent legal arguments. I am a columnist."

In that column, I admitted that "I had spent almost a decade doing little more than fighting prisoners and assaulting guards, until I somehow found the strength to turn my anger into something positive."

But, I went on to argue, "No longer confined to an existence that the prison subculture glorifies, my intellect rather than ruthlessness is the basis for self-respect. This is the essence of rehabilitation."

This is the narrative that I tried to focus upon to prevent being consumed by worry over psychological methodologies that were, quite frankly, a mystery to me. But worrying was becoming all too easy. In doing research to understand the legal landscape governing the authority vested in parole boards, the case law that I read further unsettled me.

Across the U.S., the release of a prisoner who is serving an indeterminate life sentence is often "subject entirely to the discretion of the Board, which may parole him now or never."[3] Therefore, a prisoner has an *opportunity* to be freed—but he may never have an opportunity to *be* free.

As for determining whether a prisoner is rehabilitated, parole boards assess "a multiplicity of imponderables, entailing primarily what a man is and what he may become rather than simply what he has done."[4]

Thus, parole can be denied "for a variety of reasons" that involve nothing more than "informed predictions as to what would best serve [correctional goals] or the safety and welfare of the inmate."[5]

All of this reading was chilling. Given the "multiplicity of imponderables" involved in this decision making, it seemed parole boards could do damn near anything.

Although the standard for parole eligibility is less discretionary when (as here) the governing statutes require prisoners to be freed unless a preponderance of the evidence shows that a disqualifying condition is present, in the final analysis, how a parole board *weighs* the evidence is entirely subjective.

Educated guesses and static risk assessments are all that most parole boards are left with. As a consequence, little has changed in the 50 years since the Washington Supreme Court gave voice to the mindset of parole boards:

[A]lthough releasing a convicted felon on parole may be beneficent and rehabilitative and in the long run produce a social benefit, it is also a risky business. The parole may turn loose on society individuals of the most depraved, sadistic, cruel and ruthless character who may accept parole with no genuine resolve for rehabilitation nor to observe the laws and customs promulgated by the democratic society, which in the process of self-government granted the parole.[6]

This begs the question: How can a parole board with any degree of certainty utilize a rational means to separate prisoners who are "depraved, sadistic, cruel and ruthless" from those who pose little risk to public safety?

Psychological evaluations to measure a prisoner's recidivism risk are one way to go about the process. In fact, they are mandated for Washington State prisoners affected by *Miller v. Alabama* and its progeny.

Prisoners just like me.

Which leads us back to my pre-parole hearing wariness about psychological risk assessments.

On which side of the coin would I fall after undergoing such an analysis?

Rehabilitated or likely recidivist?

This question was resolved for me on Nov.7, 2017, when the Indeterminate Sentence Review Board informed me:

The Board commends Mr. Bourgeois for completing a significant amount of programming. However, the Board has determined that he does not meet the statutory criteria for release at this time for the following reasons. Mr. Bourgeois has been assessed in his most recent psychological evaluation at a 'Moderate to High' risk to reoffend. Additionally, he has a history of serious violence while in prison, to include two felony assaults against Corrections Officers during his prison stay. Also, Mr. Bourgeois' offense is particularly heinous as it was a revenge killing against victims of a crime for which they had been willing to testify in court to assist in securing a conviction of their perpetrator, Mr. Bourgeois' brother.

And that was the end for me: The parole board took note of the good but was primarily influenced by the bad—and ugly.

Since this decision was reached, I have come to understand the methodology behind the WDOC psychologist's finding that I represent a *"Moderate to High* risk to reoffend" if conditionally released. Indeed, my discovery gives insight into the difficulty in assessing the recidivism risk of those who have spent decades confined for crimes that they committed when they were minors.

Since there is no large-scale data specific to the parole outcomes of prisoners like me, psychologists within WDOC rely upon the Violence Risk Appraisal Guide (VRAG) which was constructed and validated on a cohort comprised mostly of white Canadian male forensic patients.

Further, its revised edition (VRAG-R) relies upon a sample of individuals who, for the most part, either pleaded or were found not guilty by reason of insanity and spent an average of four years imprisoned.

The VRAG-R is designed to measure the risk of future violence by those who committed their instant offense when they were *adults* —not adolescents—and, as Dr. John Monahan, a preeminent expert on risk assessments, explains:

[T]here comes a point at which the sample to which an actuarial instrument is being applied appears so fundamentally dissimilar to the sample on which it was constructed and originally validated [ ] that one would be hard pressed to castigate the evaluator who took the actuarial estimate as advisory rather than conclusive.[7]

The VRAG-R scoring sheet, for instance, gives higher points if a person did not live with their parent(s) until they were at least age 16, are unmarried, and their crime(s) took place before they were age 26. These strikes are therefore baked in the cake when assessing those who are confined as adolescents because, ultimately, the assessment does not account for the fact that "children are different."[8]

Notwithstanding the efficacy of utilizing the VRAG-R to assess the potential risk I pose to public safety—as I wrote in the beginning —my history provided the means for crafting a narrative to support either keeping me confined permanently, or setting me free.

I just happened to fall within the category of those believed to be cloaking their criminogenic propensities.

I am still coming to terms with the notion that I am a likely recidivist.

I don't know if I will be able to get over this.

Having been denied parole after 25 years of confinement for crimes committed when I was 14, I can now envision the day when all I will have to live for is writing my monthly columns for *The Crime Report*.

—Jan. 22, 2018

3

'EVERY PRISONER IN AMERICA SHOULD BE AS ANGRY AS ME'

Jeremiah's pessimism didn't last long. He was soon preparing himself for a new hearing with the parole board, spending more hours in the prison law library, where he developed material for a research article that was accepted by the Ohio State Journal of Criminal Law. His lawyers and advisers, however, warned him that publication might imperil his campaign to free himself. It was well-meaning advice, but Jeremiah couldn't accept it. In a column published six months later, he explained why.

Although I have been confined since the age of 14, I found a way to meaningfully contribute to society.

I did this—and still do it—through my writing.

Often, as author Robert A. Ferguson writes in *Inferno: An Anatomy of American Punishment*[1], when prisoners write about the nature of imprisonment, "the oversight of officialdom produces a tortured language of evasion...[and the] fear over what authorities might do in response, distort what can be written."

However, the columns and critiques that I have published over the years illustrate that, as yet, potential repercussions have not been a deterrent.

The most recent example of my resistance (or perhaps foolishness) is a paper I wrote, entitled *A Janus-Faced Approach: Correctional Resistance to Washington State's Miller-Fix.*

In this paper, I argue that the Washington Department of Corrections is unlawfully detaining prisoners who have spent 20-plus years confined for violent offenses that they committed prior to age 18 and, due to changes in the state's sentencing laws, are entitled to be released—at least, according to my statutory analysis.

Prior to completing the final revisions, several of my lawyers advised me to abandon publication. They believed it was too risky due to my forthcoming parole hearing.

Their arguments can be distilled to the following.

First, I come across too angry, which is a terrible impression to make because correctional administrators view such prisoners negatively—and therefore, in some way, may act capriciously towards me.

Second, I give the impression that I feel entitled to be released, and parole boards take offense when prisoners act as if they are owed something.

Allowing this paper to be published before my next parole hearing, as one lawyer explained in an email to my fiancée in an effort to convince her to dissuade me, "significantly increases the chances that he is not let out and is a very, very, VERY bad idea."

One of the journal editors even felt compelled to add to the warning. Here's a partial account of our correspondence:

Dear Mr. Bourgeois: As you probably know, your attorneys also contacted us with their concerns about publishing your commentary. The position of us here at the Journal is that the decision about whether to publish rests entirely with you as the author.

We at the Journal are happy to publish now, delay publication for as long as you would like, or not publish at all. I just wanted to make sure you understood all of the possibilities. Let us know how you want us to proceed.

My response:

Hello: In my commentary I wrote that part of surviving a life sentence involved my decision to "study the law continuously, for with such knowledge I could help not only myself, but others confined with me, by seeking to hold our keepers accountable when they acted arbitrarily or capriciously." There are countless prisoners currently being affected by the practices and policies that I am highlighting. Therefore, I am going to act in conformity with the decision I made over a decade ago. Please proceed with publication as scheduled. Best regards and my thanks to all of you. I apologize if any of you were made to feel as though you were caught in an ethical dilemma.

The paper was published,[2] but I want to address what I believe lies behind the concerns that my writing could put my potential freedom in jeopardy. Namely, the pernicious notion that prisoners have no *right* to be frustrated, bitter or resentful about their imprisonment; and that retribution and incapacitation have exceeded the bounds of what is legitimate for purposes of punishment.

If *you* were ever confined for crimes that you committed in your youth, and decades later your reformation proved to be a success, it is unimaginable to me that you would not then be upset at having to continue to spend your life in darkness.

For those who have been blessed to have never experienced this earthly perdition, here is a thought experiment.

Imagine that your reckless actions resulted in you being involuntarily committed to a mental hospital, perhaps because an un-diagnosed injury to your prefrontal cortex negatively affected regions of your brain that are "implicated in processes of long-term planning, regulation of emotion, impulse control, and the evaluation of risk and reward...."[3]

For years thereafter, you shuffle down the hospital hallways dressed inappropriately, at times throw feces like a monkey, and abide by patient rules and norms that—to those in authority—are prima facie evidence that you are crazy.

One patient stabs another.

The victim falls at your feet.

You are not bothered in the least.

An orderly gets assaulted trying to restrain the assailant, and you find it amusing.

You too engage in such conduct in the grips of your insanity.

Then, one day after years of therapy and neural regeneration, you finally snap back to reality. You realize how foolish you look with your hospital pants hanging below your waistline, so you start to wear them properly. You perceive that violence is almost always unnecessary and vow to live your life peacefully. From this day forward, you begin to conduct yourself in a manner that is consistent with society's rules and expectations.

Yet, in spite of this, you remain stuck in that mental hospital surrounded by patients who, for the most part, pose a threat to themselves and others.

Regularly, you bear witness to how they abuse one another.

You see orderlies mistreat prisoners and act unprofessionally.

Staff also speak to you as if you were still crazy.

Such is life for a prisoner serving an indeterminate sentence who is fit to rejoin society, but must remain confined because the powers that be believe it is more likely than not he will commit a criminal offense if released.

I can assure you, it is a miserable existence.

Were you to remain imprisoned long after you believed your reform was complete, you too would be angry if—like me—you are utterly convinced that if set free you would be a productive member of the community.

Why would you not be moved to anger living in a place where the weak are extorted and preyed upon sexually?

Why would you not be incensed when prisoners balkanize into racial cliques and ferment unrest?

No one with a sense of morality and the capacity to feel empathy could, in my view, remain unmoved when he cannot escape "a cold and cruel place, populated by selfish, sinister people."[4]

It makes *me* angry *and* anxious. I refuse to cloak the former when I reveal the latter in writing about my life spent in confinement. The righteousness of such anger seems to be self-evident.

As for the sense of entitlement that I supposedly evince—to be clear—I have never expressed that I am entitled to be freed. I am serving an indeterminate sentence which, by its nature, means the duration of my confinement is subject to discretionary decision making.

Still, while I am not entitled to be freed, I will continue to believe that remorse, reform and a quarter century of imprisonment warrants setting me free.

I will continue to wish, as I wrote in a blog posting last June, that "every prisoner in America would become as angry as me; that they would allow its "combustible nature to propel their rehabilitation and forge a new destiny."[5]

My next parole hearing will be in July 2019. We will then see whether decision makers, as my lawyers believe, "base their moral judgments, including those concerning punishment, on their feelings," and those feelings are not always morally justified.

—July 2, 2018

4

PRETENSE, PRISON, AND THE FREE WORLD

In one of his more trenchant columns, Jeremiah addressed an issue that he assumed, despite his hopes to the contrary, that he would never face —re-engaging with family and friends outside. His musings led him to think about the policy of Washington corrections authorities to stage "family-friendly" events inside penal institutions under the thinking that they will motivate prisoners to change their behavior when they are released.

Pretense—the attempt to make something that is not the case appear to be true. It's the word that comes to mind when so-called family-friendly events take place at the facility in which I am confined.

Every six to eight weeks, the visiting room at Stafford Creek Corrections Center in Washington State is reserved for prisoners who (due to their good behavior) are allowed to attend special events such as Family Fun Night, the Back to School Event, Summer Family BBQ, and the Significant Women's Event.

On any other visitation day, the rules of decorum are quite restrictive.

Hands must remain above the table and, if intertwined, cannot move above the wrist. Prisoners are only allowed to briefly hug and kiss their visitor at the beginning and end of the visit. And as for the children, they have little entertainment other than a small play area with a television to babysit them.

In contrast, the atmosphere is far less repressive during these special family events. Prisoners can embrace the "significant women" in their life without repercussions. They can frolic with their kids outside in the sunshine, and everyone can engage with other visitors' families in wholesome activities.

Sounds awesome if you're stuck in the penitentiary—and it is.

Still, you might wonder, "What kinds of prisoners attend these events?" Devoted fathers who are anxious to get back to raising their children properly? Faithful partners who treat the women in their lives with reverence?

Of course not—let's be serious.

For the most part they were absent from their children's lives or, worse yet, negligent parents. They were philanderers who had many women in the free world convinced that their relationship was exclusive.

Pretense—all pretense.

In spite of this, many prisons hold family events under the belief that maybe—just maybe—such interactions will strengthen a prisoner's relationship with his loved ones and, in turn, better enable him to transition successfully into society.

In fact, it is well understood that the quality of social support that is available to a prisoner upon release impacts his likelihood of returning to the penitentiary.

For instance, the recidivism rate for ex-offenders who stayed in homeless shelters post-release was increased by 17 percent in one large-scale study.[1] The reality is that trying to find employment with no place to sleep is a daunting feat.

As one former prisoner explained to researcher Keesha M.

Middlemass in *Convicted and Condemned: The Politics and Policies of Prisoner Reentry*:

> *When you ain't got a place to sleep, you ain't thinking about nothing else, you only can think about a place to sleep. You sure ain't thinking about voting and stuff like that. Maybe you think about a job to get a place to sleep, maybe, but really nothing else matters except where you goin' sleep tonight.*[2]

As for family members opening their home to prisoners once they are freed, many are sympathetic—but nevertheless unwilling to tolerate the intrusion of parole officers into their residence to interfere with their peace and tranquility.

In other cases, those in the free world have become disconnected from their imprisoned family member and, frankly, had enough of them due to their years of offending.

When prisoners have nowhere to go and no one awaiting them upon release, recidivism is increased. As Middlemass explains, the "effects of homelessness and weak family bonds" in conjunction with a "lack of social capital among [ex-offenders] exacerbates negative reentry outcomes."

As such, there is a rational basis for prisons to host events aimed at strengthening the bonds between prisoners and their families, even if many of the prisoner attendees were deadbeat dads who treated women shabbily.

It is, so it seems, better that we go home to our "significant women" and children that were treated so poorly, than to end up homeless and on the precipice of reoffending.

There is a flip side to this. As with many things in life there are winners and losers; and, in this instance, those on the short end of the stick are often the children who are now put at risk.

Children whose fathers have a penchant for beating the women in their lives are 60 percent more likely to engage in serious youth violence than children who do not bear witness to domestic violence.[3]

Children who do not have their physical and emotional needs

met due to neglect have a greater risk for adult violence than if they were physically abused instead.[4]

Children whose fathers fail to provide guidance and structure do not develop self-control and, as a consequence, are more prone to aggression, according to psychologist Ervin Staub.[5]

This is what the future will bring when many prisoners enter their children's household upon being released. Let's not pretend otherwise.

We know who we're dealing with.

My life illustrates the most extreme example of what can unfold when a child is under the care and influence of such men.

Growing up, my alcoholic father was a sphinx who never fulfilled my emotional needs. He broke my mother's jaw and let her drive herself to the hospital when I was an adolescent. He used to drop me off in the middle of the night on the corner in the projects knowing that I was selling crack and carrying weapons in the process.

By the age of 14, I was confined for murder and I have not set foot on the streets since.

Sometimes a child is better off without any father in his life, rather than one who "parents" like this.

Far too many prisoners' lives have been defined by irresponsibility, violence, drug addiction, or just plain ignorance. Moreover, research reveals that maladaptive behaviors—from violence to child neglect—become family scripts that are conveyed both verbally and by example from one generation to the next as "parents reenact patterns of caregiving they experienced as children," according to Susan Crockenberg.[6]

Prisoners need only review their family scripts to see the truth in this.

One should therefore wonder why prison officials take pains to increase the prospect that the welcome mat will be laid out for prisoners upon release—knowing full well there is a high probability that they are hazardous to their children's wellbeing.

Then again, the Department of Corrections is concerned with

reducing prisoners' likelihood of re-offending as opposed to reducing the likelihood that children will become offenders.

Indeed, maybe ensuring that the next generation of convicts is developing properly is an ingenious way to ensure one's job safety.

—*Oct. 6, 2017*

5

THE 'EXTRAORDINARY' ORDINARY PRISONER

Statistics suggest that the number of inmates who commit a new crime after release is rare. But the prospect fills parole boards—and politicians who must deal with the resulting popular backlash—with dread. In 2017, three Washington State inmates whose life sentences had been commuted separately went on to commit crimes after their release. For Jeremiah that was an ominous development, but it was also an opportunity to raise questions about the nature of a corrections system that allowed "the wrong prisoners to go free."

Imagine the public outcry in your state if the following was to take place.

Three recidivists manage to get their sentences of life without parole commuted. One of them proceeds to smoke methamphetamines in a drug rehab facility and is swiftly sent back[1] to the penitentiary. The second goes on a robbery spree[2] while residing in a work release facility where he was supposed to be preparing to successfully rejoin society.

Then the third, shortly after reintegrating into the community, murders somebody.[3]

Of course, it is safe to assume that anyone involved in setting these three individuals free would pay a high price, politically.

Not in the State of Washington, where these men were granted clemency based on "extraordinary" circumstances, according to standard practice, and where the elected officials and political appointees involved in the men's release have somehow skated by with impunity.

There has been no public backlash against them. There have been no sensational stories on official negligence or incompetence.

I find that amazing.

It is also disappointing—at least insofar as it has enabled those invested in maintaining the status quo to proceed as if there are no systemic problems with the clemency process that enabled these men to be freed.

Each of these incidents highlights the wrongheadedness of an evaluation process that gives more credence to the recommendations of prosecutors and judges over any other piece of evidence.

To understand that process, consider the case of Arthur Longworth,[4] age 53, who has been confined since the age of 18 after he was convicted and sentenced to life without parole in 1984, for killing a woman during a robbery.

In the years since, he became a college graduate. He learned Chinese and Spanish. He became an award-winning writer.

Yet when Longworth went before Washington State's Board of Pardons and Parole, seeking a recommendation for a sentence commutation after having served 27 years, prosecutors maintained that his petition should be denied because the circumstances did not meet the "extraordinary" standard necessary to merit a recommendation for the governor to commute a prisoner's sentence.

The Board agreed.

The reason, which can be gleaned by watching several of such hearings, is that the meaning of "extraordinary" is not simply *very unusual and remarkable* as the term is defined in a dictionary.

Rather, it has come to mean *a very unusual and remarkable* **case**.

Quite simply, the meaning has been restricted in practice so that it has nothing to do with the person seeking relief. As I wrote last February in *The Crime Report*,[5] with respect to the clemency process:

There is nothing extraordinary about reform in the eyes of this Board. What is deemed to be extraordinary is when a prosecutor or sentencing judge supports granting clemency.

Now look at the cases of Scott Worton, David Conyers and Stony Rivers—the men who committed crimes after their sentences were commuted by the same board.

Each had been sentenced to life terms after being "Struck Out" in the 1990s under Washington's Three Strikes law.

Worton was fortunate enough to have a judge afflicted by judicial regret. Upon retiring 20 years after imposing Worton's mandatory sentence of life without parole, he enlisted high-powered attorneys to bring Worton's case before the Board and, more importantly, personally advocated that Worton be set free.

Conyers and Rivers were blessed to have an elected prosecutor who had a change-of-heart with respect to certain Three-Strike cases.

Upon taking office, the prosecutor, Dan Satterberg, reviewed those Three Strikes cases that were successfully prosecuted during his predecessor's tenure, and eventually concluded that a handful of the convicted offenders had suffered an injustice. Conyers and Rivers were among the fortunate few whose criminal histories were no longer believed to be egregious enough to merit dying in prison.

Therefore, when these men went before the Board seeking relief, the King County Prosecutor's Office did not dispute that their cases were extraordinary.

Yet, judging by their lives after confinement, none of them was in the least "extraordinary."

In truth, Worton, Conyers and Rivers each fit the prototype of a middle-aged prisoner who had been whiling away for decades doing what was necessary to get through their "time" drama-free.

Unlike Longworth, these men's lives were defined by mandatory Department of Corrections programs in Washington State, such as working in prison industries or earning a GED. Their free time was spent playing cards, watching reality television shows, exercising, and gossiping.

They were as ordinary as can be. Nothing was unusual or remarkable about them, other than that one day a criminal justice official with prestige agreed that they should be set free to undo what time has revealed to be an inequity.

Call it official soul cleansing; or rather, the enema that can set the most ordinary of prisoners free.

Objectively, were one to assess the likelihood that these three-strikers would take another swing versus Arthur Longworth's prospects for success if released, nobody who takes public safety seriously would recommend keeping Longworth confined and setting these three men free.

Prosecutors and tough-on-crime advocates usually turn such incidents into a call for wholesale action to lock people up or keep offenders imprisoned for increasingly longer durations—yet this "law and order" contingent has been curiously quiet.

On its face, this silence makes no sense.

But there is a method to their madness.

Bait-and-Switch Reform

Washington State faces a serious problem. In 2010, The Washington Supreme Court held that the State was failing to fulfill its duty to provide children with basic education.

The remedy: Money.

The amount: Billions.

Prior to this judicial decision, there had been a nascent movement championing comprehensive criminal justice reform, especially as it relates to providing long-term offenders an opportunity for early release.

Lawmakers and officials were slow to jump on board. However, as this deadline approached and neither political party has been able to agree on the best way to meet the Court's mandate to adequately fund basic education, there has been a growing realization that a substantial portion of the budget would have to be redirected if Washingtonians, true to form, reject tax increases.

Ergo—reform is on the horizon for the Department of Corrections.

Advocates for prison reform have thus been pushing for the passage of legislation known colloquially as "Second Chance"[6], which would give prisoners who have served lengthy terms of confinement an opportunity to be released by a parole board or a new Community Review Committee.

For years, these bills could not even garner a subcommittee hearing.

But these days, it is clear the momentum is on the side of those who are threading the needle between fiscal responsibility and mercy, and thus argue that releasing prisoners who are believed to no longer pose a serious threat to public safety is a sound public policy.

This is where the "law and order" contingent comes in. They see where things are heading. So, rather than oppose such efforts they propose an alternative.

A *robust* clemency process.

As conceived, the Board would be expanded so that a greater number of cases could be reviewed. In so doing, the *Second Chance* that reformers are advocating would be achieved without the necessity of structural reform within the criminal justice system.

It is pure trickery.

In reality, this alternative approach is simply a means to ensure that the gates of Washington prisons do not swing open too widely, for only a small minority of prisoners can afford the legal representation necessary to garner a clemency hearing.

Moreover, prosecutors are in the driver's seat with respect to recommendations for clemency because their opinions are tantamount to declarations from the burning bush.

Like Moses, the Board obeys.

It is this type of reform that they are willing to get behind: A review process that enables prosecutors to determine what should be deemed extraordinary enough to merit relief, and that leaves the prospects of clemency nothing but a fantasy to most prisoners due to their indigence.

In the end, it would be more of the same—with a different veneer.

Yet no matter the review process, the ultimate objective is to accurately determine if a prisoner would be likely to reoffend if set free. This is a difficult task, undoubtedly.

But if I had to choose among the lifers who have served time with me, I would surely free an Arthur Longworth before a prisoner whose extraordinary nature amounts to nothing more than a public official's belief that a prisoner is worthy of mercy.

—April 2, 2018

6

WHY ISN'T THERE A #METOO FOR IMPRISONED WOMEN?

The #MeToo campaign for women who were victims of sexual assault or harassment gained national headlines through 2017 and 2018, drawing into its orbit some of the most powerful men in U.S. entertainment and politics. But one group of victims had escaped notice, according to Jeremiah.

I am so glad that I'm not a woman—in prison.

Women were worse off than men before coming to prison—and are worse off while they are imprisoned. This was made clear to me after recently reading Joanne Belknap's *The Invisible Woman: Gender, Crime and Justice.*[1]

To illustrate this dichotomy, allow me to contrast my journey from the free world to the penitentiary with a reimagined female version of me—a female whose life exemplifies those captured in Belknap's treatise.

When I was a boy, I experienced supervisory and emotional neglect from my parents and witnessed domestic violence between them. I was emotionally abused by my father. I observed my brother being abused by my father and grandmother. And I suffered physical abuse at the hands of my brother as he paid it forward.

This childhood trauma heightened my risk for subsequent offending. By the age of 14, I was a promiscuous, marijuana-smoking runaway. Before turning 15, I was locked away in a juvenile detention facility.

All of that is terrible. Yet, had I been a young girl, my life would probably have been much more unpleasant.

According to a study cited by Belknap of youth confined in Pennsylvania, girls are eight times more likely than boys to have been sexually abused, and to have used heroin; six times more likely to have used cocaine; five times more likely to have had a sexually transmitted disease; and twice as likely to have lived in a group home before enduring a lengthy stay in a juvenile detention facility.

Editor's Note: The study referenced above can be found in: Biswas, B., & Vaughn, M. G. 2011. "Really Troubled Girls: Gender Differences in Risky Sexual Behavior and its Correlates in a Sample of Juvenile Offenders." Children & Youth Services Review 33: 2386-2391.

Before the *real me* was actually locked away, I had run away from home at the age of 13 and survived by a combination of wits and ruthlessness. I sold crack cocaine to purchase fast food when I was hungry, and also used my crack money to pay for motel rooms (using adult drug addicts as my proxy) so, during the night and early morning, I would have a warm place to sleep.

Had I been a girl during this period, I would have likely been selling my pubescent body on the corner rather than crack cocaine and bedding down with grown men on a well-worn motel mattress. Belknap highlights that childhood sexual victimization and trauma are risk factors for later prostitution; and, all too often, this is the only viable means for a young girl to make it—on her own—on the streets.

As for the heroin, as a girl, I would be eight times more likely than a boy to be using—undoubtedly as a means to self-medicate away the depression induced by my past abuse and neglect, and my present circumstances.

Back to the *real me*.

When I reached the penitentiary, I quickly realized that violence and the threat of it was necessary to prevent predators from using me for ill purposes. Extortion was something that I could conceive being a possibility if I was weak. However, the notion of being sexually assaulted by those who surrounded me was, quite frankly, terrifying.

Still, this fear would have been nothing new if I was a female arriving in the penitentiary. During my time in juvenile custody, as a young lady, I would have been six times more likely than a young man to be sexually assaulted by a staff member, and twice as likely to have been sexually abused by another female in custody, according to Belknap.

While the penitentiary is a terrible place to be, at least the *real me* has had plenty of visits over the years with those who love me. My family members have come to visit regularly throughout my confinement. More recently, I am often seen in the crowded visiting room at Stafford Creek Corrections Center enjoying my fiancée's company.

But once again, I'm a man.

Rest assured, things would be much different if I was the opposite sex, and the Washington Corrections Center for Women was my place of confinement. Reason being, women get fewer visits than men who are imprisoned because of, among other things, according to Belknap, "[t]he different values families place on the male members (husbands, fathers, sons, and brothers) as opposed to the female members (wives, mothers, daughters, and sisters)."

As for my baby's father accepting a collect call or coming to see me on visiting day—forget about it. If he's not in prison, getting plenty of visits, he's probably running around with some other "bitch." As for my daughter, she's being raised by the same people who abused and neglected me, and who set me on my path to prostitution and the penitentiary.

Such is life for too many women in the prison system.

Women's voices have been drowned out by the screams of the men who have come to define mass incarceration in this country.

My point in presenting this alternate reality is to posit this: Why is there so little interest in women and girls in confinement? To me, it seems as if their voices have been subsumed by the screams of the men who have come to define mass incarceration in this country.

Far too many people fail to recognize that when the criminal justice net was widened, females were not simply caught and released like fish unfit to eat. They too were shackled and shunted to jails and penitentiaries.

In fact, while men's imprisonment rates increased by 7.25 times from 1960 to 2011, Belknap notes, the rate of incarceration for women increased 14.1 times during the same period.

For this reason, I find it ironic that while women were marching across the country last month protesting things like gender inequality, nothing was said in the media about all these women behind bars.

Women in prison are twice as likely to have histories of childhood physical or sexual abuse than women in the general public, and 37 percent of women in state prison are rape victims.[2]

There are no #MeToo's for imprisoned women. Just "pill-line," pat-searches and, if they are lucky, a little commissary when the food in the chow hall is disgusting.

The truth is, in the realm of public opinion, as with the criminal justice system, once a person transforms into an "offender," even a traumatic history of childhood victimization does not mitigate their culpability.

Having not been freed since I was locked away in that juvenile detention facility during George H.W. Bush's presidency, I know this is the reality. But please stifle your shock at my adverse life circumstances. This isn't about me.

Keep in mind, females all too often are the ones getting the short end of a very short stick when it comes to crime and punishment. That is just the way it is.

Hence, despite all that I have been through, I am blessed.
To be a man.

—Feb. 26, 2018

7

'THEY'RE NOT MONSTERS': THE ROOTS OF YOUNG GIRLS' VIOLENCE

Jeremiah continued his focus on incarcerated women with another column a few months later that addressed the plight of a group he believed had experienced even more trauma at the hands of the justice system than he had: young girls.

When I was in my early teens, there were girls in the public housing project near my home who were as well known to the police as the boys who committed crimes with me. Just like us delinquent boys, these young ladies were quick to "get down" or, rather, to lash out violently.

The difference was that their target was typically a girl who was dissing them or a woman who unwittingly provoked them while they were out roaming the city.

During my frequent stays in the local juvenile detention center, I saw similar girls cycle through who were adjudicated for crimes that were just as serious as those committed by the boys who were confined.

In hindsight, I can see that social workers saw me as an at-risk youth in need of intervention; juvenile justice personnel viewed me as an offender in need of confinement; and prosecutors influenced by the Super Predator theory perceived me as a budding sociopath destined for the penitentiary.

But personally, I often wonder what lay behind the offending of the girls who—like me—were perpetually truant, ran away frequently, stole cars and used drugs, and at their worst, committed assaults and batteries.

Judith A. Ryder gives insight into such girls' deviance in *Girls & Violence: Tracing the Roots of Criminal Behavior*.[1]

Before delving into Ryder's thesis, it is worth taking the time to highlight some vignettes from the structured interviews that she conducted with dozens of girls who were confined in a long-term juvenile detention center. These girls were primarily black and Hispanic, their ages ranged from 14 to 16; they were raised in broken homes and foster care; and had committed assaults and robberies.

Here is Elena, age 14, sharing her theory on the pragmatic use of a knife during a fistfight:

If I'm 5'4", if a girl was like 6'2" and I can't really reach her face to fight her, and she just constantly punching me in my face and I'm hitting her but it's not working, I would just pull out a blade and just stab her in her side or something like that so she'll come down (Ryder: 136).

And here, also, is 14-year-old Adele, manifesting her need for respect when explaining why she attacked a woman on the street:

We was walking on some block...going to the train station. This lady, she was walking by, so we was like, spread out, she got to say "excuse me" to get by.... So we spreaded out and the lady had bumped me. I turned and was like, "what you doing." She was drunk and come out of her face and was like "you black bitch." So, I looked at her and I just swung on her (Ryder: 139).

Then there is vengeful 15-year-old Lisa, describing why she and her sister assaulted two small children whom they were babysitting after becoming angry at being misled by the children's mother that she would return later that evening:

[These kids' momma] didn't come back for a whole weekend, so, me and my sister got mad. So we got 'um...turned on the hot water.... We had burnt their hands.... Cause I was mad that she didn't, she didn't even, she didn't even come in, she didn't even call (Ryder:144).

Undoubtedly, reading such accounts is enough to make most people queasy. Yet Ryder does not share them for shock value. These girls' narratives are important to criminology because neither official data nor media accounts illuminate what drives such behavior.

"Calculating the number of offenses or sensationalizing individual acts fails to appreciate the context in which violence occurs or the underlying mechanisms that help propel it," Ryder explains (4). Therefore, in order to better understand such girls' violent behavior, one must "investigate the social and psychological contexts of the girls' lives before they became violent criminals" and take into account "the role of families, communities, and social institutions in the production of violence" (Ryder:5).

The Ingredients for Deviance

Ryder identifies four primary motivations for these girls' violent acts: the need for respect, the desire for vengeance, self-defense or the defense of others and, to a lesser extent, financial gain.

However, the underlying factors that help propel these girls' violent behavior is connected to their disrupted attachments and traumatic histories. In Ryder's view, the "substantial and cumulative losses and victimizations that such girls experience...interfere with the formation of attachment relationships and diminish the capacity to think about and empathize with the mental state of others" (Ryder:147-48).

This "attachment based model of female-adolescent violence" (Ryder:16) is central to Ryder's findings.

When it comes to attachment, she explains:

Children with sensitive, responsive caregivers develop secure attachment and a positive working model of themselves and others....

The early and ongoing experience of having been understood in the context of a secure attachment relationship develops within children a capacity to understand and interpret the behaviors of others in terms of the underlying intentional mental states [...] If attachment is insecure, healthy behaviors...are impaired. Children whose caregivers are unable to provide a sense of security tend to view themselves and others negatively, and their ability to accurately perceive the mental states of others may be diminished [...] When a caregiver's insensitivity is pervasive, the child's normal anger response may turn to aggression.... (Ryder:27).

Worse yet, the girls in this study not only suffered from insecure attachments, they were also plagued by "a litany of victimizations and losses to which they were exposed in their neighborhoods and homes" (Ryder:65).

Violence in the girls' neighborhoods "was widespread and touched all residents" (Ryder:65). It could erupt in a manner that was "public and random" (Ryder:69). But even in times of calm, there was no sense of security, because violence was "just beneath the surface or around the corner" (Ryder:67).

The girls' homes were also "a significant site of danger" (Ryder:73). They recount "witnessing physical violence against siblings" (Ryder:75) and recall parents and other adults "hitting them with fists, shoes, and baseball bats, and cutting them with razor blades, knives, and bottles" (Ryder:75-76).

They spoke of "sexual abuse, and of witnessing the sexual abuse of siblings and others by fathers, stepfathers, and other male relatives" (Ryder:79).

This poly-victimization—in their homes and communities—made these girls "hyper-aroused at the slightest provocation" (Ryder:141).

The fact that their violent acts manifest "the need for action over reflection" (Ryder:143) is evidenced by 14-year-old Adele's decision to swing on a woman for simply bumping into her on the street.

These girls have learned that they "must be in a constant state of readiness, prepared to act quickly to any perceived hostility" (*Ryder*:30).

With respect to the losses the girls experienced, again, they too produce traumagenic effects.

All of the girls in the study suffered loss at an early age. Namely, the physical absence of a loved one, often due to incarceration or abandonment.

The lack of the emotional support necessary to ensure their psychological wellbeing.

The loss of their homes, typically due to eviction or a change in foster care placement.

And the death of a loved one.

While it is not uncommon for youth to experience a loved one's death due to injury or illness, Ryder emphasizes that these girls' loved ones often died under socially stigmatized contexts (e.g., AIDS, drug overdose, homicide). Furthermore, their losses were compounded by the lack of "any adult assistance or support in comprehending the death" (*Ryder*:90).

Ryder highlights that these traumas resulted in the girls' employment of "a variety of maladaptive behavioral strategies" (*Ryder*:109) to defend against physical and emotional distress because, unfortunately, they never developed the coping strategies they would have had if they had received the "support and guidance of adults to assist in the bereavement and adjustment processes" (*Ryder*:109).

Not having a shoulder to cry on has consequences for a child, it seems.

And for society.

Ryder notes, "The accumulation of such losses can reinforce beliefs that life is short and violence inevitable; defensive responses may include antisocial behavior and, for some, fatalistic violence" (*Ryder*:96). Through this lens, one can see why 14-year-old Elena would find it expedient to stab a taller girl in the side to bring her down to size.

Returning to 15-year-old Lisa and her sister, who saw fit to scald the hands of two small children, in hindsight one can see that the perpetrators were victims, too. They "were victims of neglect and violence in their homes, on the streets of their neighborhoods, and in the care of social institutions created to address their needs" (*Ryder*:148).

This is not an excuse. It is just the reality.

Like other girls in the study, Lisa and her sister "had been beaten and abused, sexually violated, and then ignored, stigmatized, and penalized" (*Ryder*:148). They require "supervision and control but, as human beings, they primarily need consistent, psychologically attuned, and loving relationships," according to Ryder (*Ryder*:168).

In the end, Ryder makes a plea for there to be less "social control in the form of monitoring and punishment" and more social support in the form of "adult acceptance, affection, and guidance" (*Ryder*:168).

I wish the same for girls such as this.

Still, reflecting on the ones who used to roam the public housing project that was our former territory, I cannot imagine where any of us could have found acceptance, affection, and guidance. It was nowhere to be seen.

It is not surprising, then, that 25 years later there is a new generation of girls in that community who are perpetually truant, who run away frequently, steal cars, use drugs, and at their worst, commit assaults and batteries.

They're not monsters.

—*July 10, 2018*

8

THE ORDEAL OF GAY AND TRANSGENDER PRISONERS

*In most prisons in America, Gay and Transgender inmates face
systematic discrimination and cruelty. But the Stafford Creek facility
in Washington State has implemented model policies that address
their special needs. It evoked one of Jeremiah's rare columns of praise
for the facility where he was confined.*

One day last year, when I was enrolled in a vocational program at
Stafford Creek Corrections Center in Washington State, a classmate
of mine disappeared.

The reason behind his vanishing act was strange and, to me,
seemed to be nothing more than prisoner rumor mongering.

Here's the story. While working in the kitchen he went outside to
dump the trash and then proceeded to climb the security fence that
separated the kitchen area from the facility's industrial complex.

He wasn't trying to escape—he could only have gone from one
part of the compound to another. Instead, it appeared to be an
attempt at suicide-by-correctional officer.

Or a loss of sanity.

The rumors of his fence-climbing turned out to be true. When he was released from disciplinary segregation three weeks later, he was allowed to go back to school, and he ended up seated next to me in the classroom. I couldn't help but ask what led him to pull a stunt like that.

Voice tinged with sadness, my classmate quietly revealed to me that he was a "she"—that is, transgender. She had felt alone and depressed and had long been struggling with her sexual identity.

That was the last thing I expected to hear that morning. But once I heard this, I realized that I understood just where she was coming from—at least with respect to feeling alone and depressed.

I have long known how cruel life can be for gay, bisexual and transgender prisoners.

It can be a miserable existence.

Over the 25 years that I have been confined, the treatment they often receive is among the foul things I have had to turn a blind eye to —and it haunts me.

Most prisons are "an all-male world shaped by deprivation" and it can be especially loathsome for a prisoner who is a "gal-boy," according to prison author Wilbert Rideau.[1] He recounts how such inmates of Louisiana's Angola prison were often forced to serve as sexual outlets and "sold, traded, used as collateral, gambled off, or given away" by their "owners."

Victor Hassine, an inmate in Pennsylvania's Graterford Correctional Institution, recounts in his book, *Life Without Parole: Living in Prison Today*,[2] incidents when (presumably homosexual) staff members in Graterford isolated, overpowered and raped openly gay prisoners; and in other instances, denied "entitlements, such as positive parole reports, until victims agree to have sex."

Such is life for many gay and gender-nonconforming prisoners in America. It is a portrait of a world of depression.

From an evolutionary standpoint this is understandable.

In his book, *Origin of the Species*, Charles Darwin explains how depression "is well adapted to make a creature guard itself against any great or sudden evil."

When depression is experienced by prisoners who are already at risk because of their sexual identity, life can be worse than it otherwise would be in a correctional facility. That's because the behavior of depressed people can produce negative reactions from those around them and lead to rejection, according to research published by J. Strack and J.C. Coyne in the *Journal of Personality and Social Psychology*.[3]

Other researchers have demonstrated that once feelings of rejection become the norm, those who are depressed will begin associating with people who reinforce their poor self-image.

These are the last people a "gal-boy" should be associating with if prison safety and security is taken seriously.

Maybe this factored into why Stafford Creek began implementing policies and practices embracing gay, bisexual, transgender, and intersex prisoners.

It began last November when an LGBTI Support Group was formed with the blessing of the Associate Superintendent, Jeneva Cotton.

According to the original flyer, the purpose of the group was to foster "a supportive and educational environment" and "provide a safe platform for open dialogue about topics such as Gender Identity, Stigmas, Spirituality, Resources, Self-Acceptance [and] Incarceration."

This group is now dubbed the "Community," and one of the ground rules is to "Have Each Other's Back."

In the nine months since the Community began to meet regularly there have been noticeable changes throughout the facility.

LGBTI prisoners have been seen to wear pants so tight that—were any other prisoner wearing them—they would be rushed to the clothing room to receive pants that are looser fitting.

The appearance of some prisoners has been altered dramatically by the plucking of eyebrows and application of homemade rouge on cheeks.

Sports bras have been issued and some at times are obviously stuffed with...something.

And correctional officers can be made to perform "modified" pat searches if a prisoner proclaims *her* gender non-conformity.

Make no mistake about it: This is a social experiment under the auspices of Stafford Creek Superintendent Margaret Gilbert.

While many believe these changes are predicated on the whim of highly placed sympathizers within the state Department of Corrections, they're actually rooted in pre-existing policies and legislative decrees.

One of the purposes of punishment in the State of Washington is to "offer the offender an opportunity to improve himself or herself." The legislature has also mandated that the correctional system should treat all prisoners "fairly and equitably."

Over the years, such dictates have led to accommodations being made for prisoners besides those who are marginalized due to their sexual identity.

For instance, there was a time when African-American hair products were not sold within the DOC system, but the Black Prisoners' Caucus successfully advocated for Afrocentric conditioners and hair grease.

Non-Christian faiths are given the freedom to practice their religions even when correctional officials have reason to believe the "religion" is simply a front for a security threat group.

Muslim prisoners can even be seen every Friday at Stafford Creek wearing religious garb to their prayer service.

Ironically, many of the very prisoners who have the freedom to express their minority cultures and non-conventional religious ideologies are staunchly opposed to LGBTI prisoners having a Community with the stated vision of creating "A Positive, Pro-Social Environment that Nurtures Acceptance, Individuality & Equality."

Grumbling aside, I seriously doubt that Associate Superintendent Cotton and other administrators at Stafford Creek are simply hell bent on enforcing political correctness. There is actually an argument to be made that such policies and practices further the goal of rehabilitation.

It all comes down to programming.

According to researchers Keith O'Brien and Sarah Lawrence of the Washington State Institute for Public Policy[4], job training, vocation educational programs, and work release "produce modest but statistically significant reductions in recidivism."

Yet as Michael Lovaglia notes in his book, *Knowing People: The Personal Use of Social Psychology*, "Depression creates profound problems in the social functioning of those who suffer from it, more so than any other psychiatric disorders."[5]

My fence-climbing, transgender classmate's experience demonstrates quite clearly how prisoners' desire to take advantage of program opportunities can be inhibited when they feel alone, isolated, and are struggling with their sexual identity in a hypermasculine subculture that views them contemptuously.

Without such programming (or the ability to do so effectively), there will not be "statistically significant reductions in recidivism" for prisoners who are marginalized due to their sexual identities.

The DOC in Washington State also has an avowed commitment "to non-discrimination in offender programming" and seeks to "prevent discrimination from occurring by identifying practices and procedures that could have the effect of discrimination and take steps to eliminate the potential for discrimination."

So, for those who believe that allowing stuffed sports bras, plucked eye brows, and tight slacks is going too far simply to make some "weirdos" feel adjusted enough to program effectively—you should know that the DOC is directed to "positively impact offenders" and the Legislature believes "[a]ll citizens, the public and inmates alike, have a personal [ ] obligation in the corrections system."

In light of all this, my suggestion to the dissenters inside prison is this: Bite your tongue and consider your acquiescence a fulfillment of your personal obligation to the correctional system.

If you feel differently, go ahead and say or do the wrong thing and I promise that you will feel the full wrath of bureaucracy.

Or maybe not.

Soon there will be a new regime at Stafford Creek when Margaret Gilbert retires on September 15.

In Gilbert's farewell message she wrote, "Every time you make a decision to do the right thing you're creating a future. Every time you make a bad decision it affects someone else."

Only time will tell what the future will bring for LGBTI prisoners at Stafford Creek.

—Sept. 6, 2017

9

INSIDE PRISON, RACIAL PRIDE OFTEN LOOKS LIKE HYPOCRISY

Like the #MeToo movement, the campaign to address racial bias in the justice system and elsewhere nurtured a growing sense of empowerment and solidarity, particularly among African-American and Latinx youth across the country. Washington State prison authorities, considering it a healthy way to instill pride, build character and reduce racial tensions, encouraged inmates to develop ethnic awareness. Not surprisingly, Jeremiah was skeptical.

Prior to being confined, I had never heard of *Kwanzaa*.

I knew nothing about *Juneteenth*.

During my short time in the free world, I met nobody who celebrated such things.

Then, following my arrival at Washington State Penitentiary, a prisoner that I lived on the cellblock with offered me a "Happy Kwanzaa" card during the holiday season. I looked it over and could not hide my bemusement, and I said to him "Why the f---k would I send this to my family? We never celebrated no shit like this."

He looked at me with scorn and faux sadness, and, after letting a few seconds elapse to add emphasis to his words, replied to me by saying, "It's so pitiful that so many brothas don't know about their own heritage."

This was my first up-close encounter with someone suffering from a malady that I have since labeled "contradictory racial consciousness."

It is a mental illness that hopefully will be included in a future edition of the *Diagnostic and Statistical Manual of Mental Disorders.*

Its symptoms include the constant display of affinity for one's culture once deprived of one's liberty.

It is prevalent among men who spent their time in society killing, robbing and selling drugs in their communities; then, upon being confined, spend their time trumpeting the culture of the peoples they exploited while free.

Having lived benighted lives and accomplished nothing worthwhile through individual means, they seem to gain self-esteem by reimagining themselves as a faithful member of a culture that is worth celebrating.

African-American prisoners are not unique when it comes to this contradictory racial consciousness. Remaking oneself as a culture warrior is a popular pastime among those with different races and ethnicities.

This leads to some ironic situations.

For instance, Native Americans come to prison and grow out their hair, burn sage and don medicine bags, and take up beading —while on the streets, many were members of the Bloods and Crips or, alternatively, practiced ways no different than *The White Man.*

Mexican Americans start to espouse *Brown Pride*, read books on Cesar Chavez, and study the *Chicano Movement*; all the while engaging in gang warfare throughout the prison system with those who share their culture and resemble them—so much for *La Raza.*

Not to be left out, white prisoners will become experts on European history to add grist to their ethnocentric concepts, seemingly oblivious that their swastika tattoos would be utterly repulsive to their European kinsmen.

Strange as all of this seems, the Washington Department of Corrections (WDOC) allows prisoners such as these to hold annual events aimed at fostering cultural awareness.

Several times a year, prisoners can go to the visiting room, eat ethnic dishes with their family and friends, and watch their imprisoned brethren perform tribal dances.

I am quite serious.

Requiem for Kunta Kinte

Years ago, as sort of an anthropological study, I attended the annual *Juneteenth* celebration at Stafford Creek Corrections Center. The food was delicious; but frankly, the entertainment made me nauseous.

There was spoken-word poetry about how we need to cherish our *sistas;* never mind the fact that most of the *brothas* in attendance were in relationships with white women.

There were rappers whose lyrics on any other day of the year promoted getting money, buying kilos of cocaine, and exploiting women; but for this special occasion, they heaped praise on Malcom X, Marcus Garvey and Angela Davis.

The grand finale was the worst of it: I had to bear witness to a dozen gang members in Afrocentric garb (where it came from is a mystery) dancing to West African drumming from a sound system. These men had been allowed by some administrator to study dancers from Senegal on DVD, and they decided to mimic them as if they had arrived at Stafford Creek live and direct from the Motherland.

The honorees in attendance thoroughly enjoyed the performance. These African-American women, who were respected community activists, were enthralled. "Look at our handsome brothas," I could hear them thinking. I could not stop sneaking glances at them as I steadily ate pieces of chicken.

Finally, the show ended: The Africans morphed back into convicts; and, when all the prisoners returned to their units, many of the *brothas* who had been extolled to cherish *sistas* got into the phone line to call up the white women they were in a relationship with (myself included).

Behind the Billing of Cultural Diversity

Were you to ask a senior WDOC administrator about the purpose behind allowing such events, the answer would likely be that they further prisoners' understanding and appreciation for different cultures, and thereby reduce racial tension and conflict within WDOC facilities.

But this is fantasy, not reality.

In truth, the events testify to the fact that correctional systems across the nation operate in a state of de facto segregation, and prisoners remain the force behind maintaining this separate and equal stasis.

Consequently, you will not see Latinos eating gumbo with the *brothas* celebrating *Juneteenth*; whites will not be attending Hispanic cultural events listening to Mariachi; and blacks will not be going to any pow wows to share fry bread with Native Americans.

As for the European Day event that occurred at Stafford Creek, there might as well have been a Whites Only sign hanging above the visiting room entrance.

Quite simply, segregated activities are exactly how most prisoners want them to be.

In light of the dangerous company in a prison setting, prejudice seems inevitable. As psychologist Michael Lovaglia observes, "We are prejudiced to the extent we feel threatened or fearful."[1]

In the end, cultural celebrations in WDOC are a win-win situation for all parties. Prisoners extract events that they can participate in with their families and friends outside the presence of *the others*.

As for WDOC, it can bill itself as an agency that is open and accepting of the cultures of those whom society has rejected.

—July 26, 2018

Jeremiah Bourgeois *(Photo taken while he was imprisoned)*

Jeremiah Bourgeois after release from prison, January 2020

Stafford Creek Correctional Center (Photo courtesy Washington
Department of Corrections)

10

THE REAL NIGHTMARE OF SOLITARY

Life in prison is a little easier when you can find a good book to absorb your waking hours. But when you're in solitary, reading can become an unsettling experience.

Last year, I underwent a private forensic psychological evaluation in preparation for a parole hearing that could have set me free. Having served 25 years in confinement at that time of the evaluation, the results did not surprise me.

According to the psychologist:

Results indicate that the respondent does not currently appear to satisfy DSM-IV-TR diagnostic criteria for PTSD [Posttraumatic Stress Disorder] or ASD [Acute Stress Disorder], despite reporting a significant trauma history. Nonetheless, he does report significant levels of post-traumatic re-experiencing and avoidance, which is suggestive of post-traumatic stress that falls short of a diagnosable disorder. Individuals with such clinical presentations, although not meeting the full criteria for PTSD/ASD, may suffer considerable distress and often benefit from psychological treatment and/or pharmacotherapy.

Indeed, I often do experience "considerable distress" as recognized by the psychologist. The most recent incident during which I had to suffer through "post-traumatic re-experiencing" occurred while I was reading the prologue to *Zek: An American Prison Story.*[1]

The author, Arthur Longworth (whom I have written about before), spent the last 34 years confined in the State of Washington for a murder that he committed at the age of 18. He managed to make me nauseous with a four-page scene that most people would not have found to be anxiety-inducing.

Here is how the scene unfolds.

A prisoner is in long-term solitary confinement. For six months, he has been on isolation status, and has been allowed nothing other than some hygiene products and clothing. Down the cellblock, another prisoner has just been forcibly removed from his cell after being sprayed with mace, tazed and wrestled down into submission, trussed up with his ankles and wrists cuffed together, then carried off to another cell where he will remain naked for an indeterminate period.

Cell extraction complete, the prisoner notices a book amidst the other prisoner's blood and pepper spray-smeared bedding, which was thrown out on the tier when guards removed the former occupant's belongings.

The prisoner finds the sight uplifting, for he has not been allowed any books during the six months that he has been on isolation status.

So, he makes an improvised grappling device with thread from his underwear, a plastic comb, and several staples that he had secreted in a crack between the floor and wall; and, after numerous attempts at snagging the book as if he is fly fishing, he manages to reel in his catch and happily begins to read.

This is when my stomach got queasy, as the narrative continued with the following:

Several hours later, he let the book's cover close but continued to stare at it for some time. Any other book he would have rationed— reading a page or two at a time, holding himself to only enough per day to keep his mind from eroding, yet still have more to read for the next day—that was the way he had learned to do it in that place. He had found that it wasn't possible with this book, though. (Longworth:11).

Reading this really disturbed me.

It had been a long time since I had been in long-term solitary confinement. Given this reprieve, I had apparently suppressed these seemingly mundane experiences from my mind—and the memories came flooding back to me when reading this all-too-real work of fiction.

To find a book so good that you cannot resist the temptation to continue reading it—as if you are in the free world or the general prison population, and rationing your reading material is unnecessary to protect your sanity—is an absolute disaster when locked away in long-term solitary confinement.

Long ago, I too learned the necessity of book rationing.

From the age of 15 to 24, I spent a total of six years in isolation, confined 23 hours each day in my cell, and was only provided with two books every week.

Every time that I submitted my books to be exchanged, I spent the interim worrying that I would receive books in return that I had already read, given that there were no more than 500 books available and approximately 75 prisoners clamoring to get their hands on them.

With so few books, the longer a prisoner stayed in segregation the higher the probability that he was going to be disappointed when those books slid under the door.

Yet even when I received books that I still had not read, my feelings would soon cycle between irritation and fury because of the surprises that awaited me. Without fail, there would be random messages scrawled on the pages declaring, for instance:

Mo Money, Moe Bitches.

White Power.

Fuck the Police.

A page (or all of them) might also have every instance of the letter "b" or "c" crossed out by a gang member who decided that the inside of a book was an appropriate place to start pseudo *set tripping*.

Any page might also harbor dried, bloody mucus smeared from one end to the other or a collection of crusty boogers reminiscent of a popcorn ceiling. This biohazard, I can only assume, comes courtesy of one of the countless mentally ill prisoners stuck in segregation for being a threat to themselves or others or to the orderly operation of the facility.

However, there are worse things than having to see ignorant declarations written throughout a book by imprisoned scribes and having to avoid contamination while reading.

When one finds several pages missing from a book it is truly infuriating. Usually, I would come across a gap in the story when two characters were embraced, kissing and undressing, then...I realize some freak has ripped out the sexual encounter that I was expecting.

I used to wish all kinds of calamities would befall prisoners whose prurient interests drove them to butcher the books to obtain material for fantasizing. Yet a missing erotic scene is nothing compared to a missing ending.

Imagine reading several hundred pages of a story, engrossed in the plot, only to find that the last chapter of the book is nowhere to be seen.

This happened to me time and again.

Once, a malicious malcontent (who was probably the culprit) got a kick out of writing a message where the last chapter should have been that said, "Bet you want to know the ending. Ha Ha! Eat a dick."

There was nothing that I could do. I just put the book down, closed my eyes, laid back on the thin mattress, and had to endure the sounds of someone raging at the officers every hour that they passed by his cell.

With nothing to read, I would pace the floor hearing guys converse through the interconnected vents about their past exploits and future misdeeds.

With no book to occupy my mind, I would try to meditate as guys yelled back and forth arguing about something meaningless and threatening one another with violence if ever they got the opportunity for vengeance.

Then there is the fear that used to haunt me.

The fear that I would sleep too heavily and not make it to the yellow line at the front of the cell where I had to be standing to receive a meal to eat; and, consequently, I often awoke in a panic when I heard sounds that were similar to the food cart passing by, because I thought I had missed my meal and would have to go hungry.

The fear that made me refuse to go to recreation or shower sometimes because I had hidden some of my food in order to have something to eat during the 14 hours from dinner to breakfast—food that would be thrown away by officers as contraband if they conducted a cell search when I was getting fresh air or bathing.

There is no doubt that years of experiencing such things—on a daily basis—had a profound effect on my psyche, and exacerbated the damage being done from being imprisoned in my teens.

It is manifest when I live in my head for hours on end, find entertainment in my imaginings, and even laugh out loud at something that amuses me.

It is illustrated when prisoners and staff members come to see that I do not need the company of others to feel complete: I can be quiet, solitary, and not bothered in the least.

Unfortunately, given the nature of imprisonment and my history, I have no doubt that if I remain confined there will eventually come a time when I am once again in solitary confinement. Rest assured, if that day arrives there is one thing that I will pray for.

A good book. A book that I have not read before. A book that is mucus and booger free, and that is complete from the beginning to the ending.

—August 7, 2018

11

WHERE BLACK LIVES (ALSO) DON'T MATTER

The racial bias that often fuels police mistreatment of African Americans has motivated a nationwide campaign for equity, accountability and transparency. But viewing the campaign through the prism of his confinement, where such problems are just as systemic, Jeremiah is skeptical that activism will produce these outcomes.

While we have come a long way since the days of endemic racial prejudice within police departments, some things seem impervious to change.

I lack the imagination to depict what it was like to have an encounter with the police—as a black male—in 1956. Yet, despite the melanin in my skin, I cannot tell you what this experience is like for a black man in contemporary America either.

My status as a convict has shaped me far more than my experiences in society, given that I have been confined since the age of 14.

Consequently, my world view is far different than many of those who share my complexion but have been fortunate enough not to have had their existence defined by mass incarceration.

Given this, I am often perplexed by African Americans who

came of age in an era when video cameras are utilized by police officers while performing their duties, and when anyone can unleash his or her cellphone to capture encounters between the police and the citizenry.

Through the lens of my television screen, I regularly see young black men and women displaying dismay, frustration and fury when their fellows suffer injustices at the hands of the police. Such encounters and their aftermath are replayed on CNN and MSNBC for the world to see.

It is a show that I have seen time and again. The faces of those leading the chorus of outrage have changed, from old-school luminaries like Jesse Jackson, Al Sharpton and Louis Farrakhan to a new generation of activists, but as far as I can tell, watching from my prison cell, the message hasn't changed.

While I have a personal interest in seeing a reduction in the probability that an unarmed black man will be shot down by the police (especially since I may be paroled, and the victim could be me), I doubt that such a result will ever be achieved in the 21st Century.

There are several reasons why I am skeptical.

First, black people continue to be seen as dangerous. As the authors of the recently updated *The Black Image in the White Mind*[1] show, the media has a long history of portraying black men as violent, and white people have been a receptive audience.

Fear of the black man is as American as apple pie—and lynching.

Fear-of-the black-man is not "taught" in police academies. The book's authors, Robert M. Entman and Andrew Rojecki, make clear that such fear is the byproduct of a cultural meme that was implanted in police officers' subconscious during their formative years—long before they chose a career in law enforcement.

This is the grim reality through which efforts to deter officers from using deadly force without justification, ranging from de-escalation training to the threat of prosecution, must be seen. They will make little difference to the black man who gets stopped and frisked, because such efforts won't change hearts and minds.

To expect otherwise is to believe black men can be made to no longer feel anxiety when confronted by the police.

As a parallel, I have watched the Washington Department of Corrections make futile attempts to change the mindset of correctional officers in order to make imprisonment less dehumanizing to those who have lost their liberty. Administrators wanted them to refer to us as "individuals" but pushback from officers resulted in the quick reimposition of "offender."

They have been instructed to log positive interactions with prisoners as opposed to only negative encounters. Yet try as they might, they cannot help but focus on the latter.

The ugly truth is that most correctional staff cannot perceive us as anything other than convicts who are *unworthy*; just as police officers are primed to see that black man as a potentially dangerous criminal.

In fact, were you to review video footage inside of prisons, you would see the same phenomenon at play. Prisoners know full well that challenging correctional officers' authority often leads to arbitrary and sometimes violent reactions. The training that these officers received—to be measured and consistent when dealing with "offenders"—often goes out the window in the face of defiance.

It comes as no surprise, then, when I see people on my television screen experience this backlash during encounters with law enforcement. Prison is just a microcosm of society.

Finally, police officers exist within a subculture that fuels negative perceptions about (primarily young) black males (and black police officers are not immune when it comes to *brothas* that fit a "profile").

I too live in a subculture that fuels a heightened level of prejudice. My prison experience has led me to believe that Chicanos feel animus towards black men. More than any other group around me, I feel unsafe when in their midst. Were I in the wrong place at the wrong time, I am convinced that I could be assaulted.

It is noteworthy that I have yet to suffer an attack. But plenty of those who look like me have fallen victim at other facilities. I therefore perceive the threat to be real and conduct myself accordingly.

Fortunately, I have the luxury of avoiding those I believe pose a threat to my safety. But police officers must confront those they perceive as their adversaries.

So, I expect that police officers will often be hostile, abrasive and aggressive. Fear and prejudice apparently make it too difficult for police to serve and protect without bias and to avoid confrontations with African-American citizens.

That such encounters occasionally escalate into violence does not surprise me in the least. That the unarmed man loses in the end is the natural order of things.

Forgive me if I seem to lack empathy. I wish the world were different.

Yet at the end of the day, protests, prosecutions and changes to policies and practices will not make black men seem peaceful and law abiding to those with guns and badges. Likewise, better training is not going to render police officers incapable of overreaction.

The new generation of African-American activists who believe in justice and equality should therefore be cautious. They should never forget that racial prejudice can erupt with little warning, if they want to be sure their last moments aren't captured on video for the world to see.

—Oct. 1, 2018

12

BEHIND BARS, RAGE CAN BE THERAPEUTIC

Correctional institutions now offer a wide range of rehabilitative programs like Yoga classes to help inmates endure their time. But during his long captivity, Jeremiah discovered that finding ways to channel quiet anger was the best survival mechanism.

Savvy prison systems such as the Washington Department of Corrections (WDOC) tout dog training programs, sustainability projects, and yoga classes to market their humane and rehabilitative environments to members of the public who are curious enough to want to know what is occurring inside of them.

Yet behind the window dressing there remains "a trace of torture in the modern mechanisms of criminal justice," and it is "enveloped increasingly by the non-corporal nature of the penal system."

Those are the words of Michael Foucault, and they apply to the institution where I am serving a life sentence, as well as to most others.

Tension between guards and inmates is all too common in correctional settings.

However, I have learned that it is prudent to cloak my anger and hostility. Being perceived by one's keepers as a malcontent can result in reprisals, especially in minimum custody facilities where the perception amongst staff is that prisoners—who have the luxury of living in less repressive settings—have too much to lose to react violently when treated unjustly.

Emboldened by this belief, many guards will not hesitate to pluck a seemingly hostile prisoner out of a crowd and pat-search them aggressively.

They will frequently search these prisoners' cells under pretexts and leave them in shambles.

They will confiscate their property illegitimately and claim it violates policy.

Staff will delay or "lose" paperwork that requires approval for prisoners to obtain jobs, schooling, and transfers to work release.

Such examples illustrate why I don a mask of equanimity. Yet for some prisoners, becoming a sphinx does not inoculate against capriciousness. Those who use writing as a means for venting their discontent and have the nerve to let those views be published can face repercussions.

To some, we were confined solely to be punished; we have no business complaining as if we are suffering injustices. They believe prisoners are working off a debt to society and, by reason of this, are unfit to feel anger that is righteous.

There is an irony to this.

In writing about the true nature of imprisonment, as opposed to lashing out, prisoners are employing the very methods that correctional systems force-feed them through cognitive behavior therapy (CBT).

For those unfamiliar with this treatment, the core premise of CBT is simple, according to an article in the *National Institute of Justice Journal*:

The way we think about situations shapes our choices, behavior and actions. If flawed or maladaptive thoughts, attitudes, and beliefs lead to inappropriate and even destructive behavior, then changing thoughts, attitudes and beliefs can lead to more appropriate, pro-social behavior.[1]

Under this rubric, the object of the *Stress & Anger Management* CBT program within WDOC is to help "offenders recognize their angry feelings, learn their causes, and deal with them in a new way—a responsible way—probably not the way they learned to deal with them in the past," according to the aptly titled *Cage Your Rage* workbook.[2]

Prisoners in WDOC are given some of the following instructions for *responsibly* managing their stress and anger:

- *Don't keep angry feelings bottled up inside. They will only cause you problems and pain.*
- *You know that built-up anger only makes a situation worse—worse for yourself and worse for others.*
- *If we don't deal with our feelings of anger, they only lead to aggression.*

In fact, caging one's rage "doesn't mean you should get rid of all your anger [because] anger does have some good uses," according to the *Cage Your Rage* script.

Every time that a prisoner manages his anger and stress by weaponizing his pen rather than beating and slashing his keepers, he proves that anger can indeed be put to good use.

As a twist, the final lesson from CBT appears to be that taking to heart the rehabilitative programing provided by WDOC can actually lead to ruin, and confirms Durkheim's view that "the essence of punishment is irrational, unthinking emotion fixed by a sense of the sacred and its violation."

In the end, the pen becomes a blade for a prisoner to perform Seppuku.

In a 2017 article in the *Punishment & Society*[3] journal, Prof. Steve Herbert recognizes that prisoners who are serving life sentences "exemplify and enact the human capacities for connection, generosity, resilience, and atonement; for these and other reasons, their experiences deserve greater consideration and discussions of punishment policy."

He is right.

—Nov. 23, 2018

13

THE 'WOMB-TO-PRISON PIPELINE'

Justice reformers focus on preventing schools from employing discipli-nary approaches that send troubled youths into the justice system. But for many young black males, the so-called school-to-prison pipeline begins a lot earlier. In one of his bleaker columns, Jeremiah reflects on his own experience before prison.

It is interesting how researchers conceive phrases and terms that capture their findings in readily accessible ways that resonate in the mind of the public. They capture a phenomenon that makes their conclusions marketable to policymakers and officials—even if the findings later prove to be (at best) misleading, or (worse yet) erroneous.

Take the bogus "superpredator" theory. Officials saw fit to prose-cute me as if I were an adult when this theory was in its infancy and sentenced me to life without parole when I was only 14 years old, under the fiction that I was irredeemable and beyond reform.

Today, I often read about a "School-to-Prison Pipeline."

The necessary materials for building a School-to-Prison Pipeline are black boys, bureaucrats, and overt and implicit bias. With this, one can create environments within schools where the "students who are most in need of support and attention from the public education system are most harmed by its impersonal mechanisms," according to *Breaking the Chains, The School-to-Prison Pipeline, Implicit Bias, and Racial Trauma.*[1]

For instance, a black male student with an intellectual, emotional or physical disability "has a 33.8 percent chance of being suspended in a given school year compared to only a 16.2 percent chance for similarly situated white males," explain the authors of *Breaking the Chains.*

The authors also say that "black boys are seen as older and less innocent" than their white same- age peers. So when "black students do indeed misbehave in class, teachers [are] more likely to see these actions as the product of a pattern when compared with White students," and this "negative stereotyping of a black student's disobedience has been associated with the black escalation effect."

This educational experience, or escalation effect, according to this line of thinking, pushes many young black males out of public schools and into the juvenile justice system and eventually—if they are as unlucky as me—into the penitentiary.

I do not doubt any of the findings of the School-to-Prison Pipeline theory. However, while the outflow of the pipeline is apparent, I disagree with where it begins.

Allow me to present the "Womb-to-Prison Pipeline."

The essential components for building this section of the pipeline are black children who were exposed, in utero, to drugs and alcohol, maternal stress, and malnourishment; then come to suffer traumatic experiences at the hands of caretakers who abuse and neglect them.

These are the adverse experiences that define the lives of countless black children who enter the public-school system. They learned to disassociate or be aggressive in order to survive their traumatic experiences and environments. Then, as explained in *Breaking the Chains*, those behaviors become "maladaptive in the school setting" and are "misinterpreted by school staff" as evidence of "ill-intentioned misbehavior."

Through this lens, one can see that our problems began in the home rather than in a school setting. Teachers are then left to corral and educate what have become, in essence, defective units.

Few liberals would dare to express such a thing.

For good reason, they are cowed by those who would cry that such a view is both politically incorrect *and* vacuous because it gives credence to the notion that black folks are responsible for everything that has befallen them throughout American history.

It is well-nigh heresy for a black *prisoner* to believe that the home front was the proximate cause of our predicament. I know this from personal experience.

In the past, I have provoked consternation and irritation by expressing these sentiments during meetings of the *Black Prisoners' Caucus*.[2] How dare I cite *our* shortcomings during a discussion on mass incarceration or miseducation—*especially* in the presence of bright-eyed white guests from the community who are our allies and potential advocates?

The implicit message is that we must always blame the system. This is the script to follow if one wishes to be accepted by their brethren and not be labeled a fool or sellout by those who are "woke."

To be clear: I believe that mass incarceration is a product of historical antecedents, contemporary policies and practices, and overt and implicit bias against African Americans by those with the power to subjugate us. Furthermore, I accept the notion that reforming the public school system can ameliorate (or at least, stop facilitating) mass incarceration.

Yet the power that lords over us initially is parental authority, and the School-to-Prison Pipeline seems to ignore this reality.

It is the abuse of *this* authority that leaves black children at the mercy of the system, whether that system endeavors to educate or incarcerate. If reducing mass incarceration is the objective, the focus should be on repairing the Womb-to-School section of the pipeline to prison.

But at the end of the day, if ignoring the man in the mirror and absolving our kin of culpability furthers criminal justice reform, so be it. I have no problem falling back and letting others articulate the *raison d'etre* for narrowing the pipeline to the penitentiary.

I am willing to do whatever is necessary to reduce the likelihood that my nephew finds himself in prison with me.

—Jan. 3, 2019

14

AMERICA'S SADDEST PRISONERS

The tragedy of opioid abuse has cut a swath through American society, with authorities desperately trying to address what is now called a "public health" epidemic. But an earlier generation of young, mostly black men who were similar victims of addiction are still languishing in prison, labeled as "super-predators" for behavior that today would likely not earn them prison time. Jeremiah observes that their plight is still largely ignored by the outside world.

There is a strange parallel between the history of the so-called "superpredator" and the conception of "dope fiends."

Not too long ago, "superpredator" was used by some criminologists to describe the emergence of what was considered a dangerous threat to public safety: A ruthless, violent criminal concealed within the body of an adolescent male, he was often black, and his habitat was the inner city.

When captured, the mantra "Adult Time for Adult Crime" supported sentencing them as if they were just as culpable as their fully matured counterparts.

The superpredator theory has long since been discredited in the outside world.

Now, there's a broad consensus among criminologists that the so-called superpredator is better understood as a youth whose crimes often reflect transient immaturity rather than irreparable corruption, and whose skin complexions encompass the color spectrum. The U.S. Supreme Court and, last year, the Washington State Supreme Court, relied upon the attendant neurodevelopmental research findings to invalidate some of the harshest penalties for the kinds of juvenile offenders once written off as unreformable superpredators.

Even heinous crimes committed by young people are now viewed through a prism that mitigates their culpability.

I was once in the superpredator category myself. I received a life-without-parole sentence for my involvement in a murder at age 14—a crime that I have regretted ever since.

But the courts' new approach gave me—and many others in similar situations—a path for hope. My sentence was amended retroactively, and I was given an opportunity to be freed. I received mercy.

But the superpredator theory still operates for a certain class of offenders. The typology describes prisoners who were immersed in the world of illicit drugs, and the stereotype is just as brutal: He (usually a he) was conceived to be a hedonistic, nihilistic hybrid, usually having dark skin, who sometimes spoke with a Hispanic accent.

Such young men represent the new version of what used to be called "dope fiends." Committing crimes to support their narcotic addition, they were targets of the "tough on crime" policies that sent so many young black men to prison in the 1980s and 1990s for long stretches of confinement.

That stereotyped version of "superpredator" now stunts the lives of thousands of inmates in U.S. prisons today who were sentenced for drug-related crimes committed when they were young.

They have largely been ignored by the growing consensus created by the nation's opioid epidemic. We all realize that the opioid epidemic in America has destroyed the lives of soccer moms and rural white teenagers just as much as it has black youths in the inner city.

The broad consensus that dealing with this crisis requires a public health approach, rather than criminal justice machinery, has spread to policymakers at federal, state and local levels.

But not to prisons.

The ameliorative approaches [to substance abuse and addiction] are only being implemented at the front end of the criminal justice system. Unlike former superpredators such as myself, mercy has yet to be applied retroactively to the sentences of opioid addicts imprisoned while they were young. Their lives are untouched by the contemporary recognition that their crimes were not simply a product of free will, opportunity and a rational calculus.

The case of Corey Irish illustrates why such former drug "superpredators" should receive relief—notwithstanding the fact that their crimes occurred long before overdosed bodies began to pile up in refrigerator trucks from West Virginia to Ohio.

Drugstore Robbery

Late in the evening of April 23, 2007, in Tacoma, Wash., Daniel Garibay was just about to turn away from the customer he finished serving through the drive-through window at Walgreen's pharmacy when he heard a loud thump on the floor behind him.

He would never forget the sound.

"I mean, I'd never heard something like that," he testified, according to trial transcripts.[1]

The sound was Corey Irish landing on the floor after he leapt over the counter. The young man immediately began demanding drugs by their generic and non-generic names.

"When he first jumped in, at first he asked for Percocet, Oxycodone, and Vicodin...then it seemed like he just wanted anything," Garibay told the jury during Irish's trial in Pierce County Superior Court.

He was stunned when Irish pulled out two trash bags and told Garibay to fill them up. According to Garibay, "They looked like forceflex bags. He told me which drugs he wanted, and then he asked me to put them in the bags after I opened the cabinet."

Meanwhile, Irish's accomplice, who stood guard over the other two employees after flashing a gun in his waistline and corralling them into the stockroom, kept apologizing.

"I'm sorry I have to do this, you know...Just be quiet," Jeanelle O'Dell recalled the accomplice saying as he made her kneel on the floor.

Mike Staten also remembered that "he kept apologizing for what he was doing, saying he wanted to be in and out."

Back in the pharmacy, Garibay had moved on to filling up a third garbage bag that Irish made him get after the two that Irish brought with him were filled to capacity. Ten minutes elapsed from the loud thump Irish made when he landed behind the counter to when he finally lifted the bags filled with childproof bottles, summoned his accomplice from the stockroom, and began to leave with his haul of prescription narcotics.

The police arrived before the men escaped from the scene. Irish was arrested with the bags of OxyContin, Percocet, Valium and Vicodin, and everything in between. His accomplice fled empty-handed and was never apprehended by the police.

During the closing arguments of Irish's trial, Sunni Ko, the deputy prosecuting attorney, rhetorically asked the jury, "Ladies and gentlemen, again, what do you think he was going to do with three bags of drugs? Do you think that he was going to keep them in his room and have it for personal use for the rest of his life?"

The notion that an addiction to prescription medication was powerful enough to make anyone do such a thing stretched belief. His intent was obviously to distribute the pills for profit, Ko argued to the jury.

The jury agreed.

At sentencing, Irish, who met the DSM-IV-TR criteria for opioid dependency, explained to the judge, "We wasn't trying to hurt anybody. We just wanted some pills. And besides...I do pop pills, constantly. That's why—not making excuses on any of that—but I mean, I do have a problem."

Irish concluded by saying, "Whether it was one bottle or 100 bottles I took, it was going to be a robbery anyway, so I mean, a thousand apologies, especially to the victims."

His mother, a high school teacher, told the judge how she had tried to convince her son to get treatment before the crime occurred. His aunt, an assistant mayor, also implored the court, writing, "Corey needs the opportunity to enter a program where he can receive help for the drug problem and counseling to get to the root of his problems."

The judge empathized with Irish's family, but she had no sympathy for Irish.

He was sentenced to spend the next quarter century in the care of the Washington Department of Corrections—a prison term that exceeds the minimum sentence a defendant would serve for committing premeditated murder.

The Paradigm Shift

Criminal justice officials in Ohio probably would not be surprised upon hearing that someone tried to steal garbage bags filled with prescription pills from a pharmacy in a robbery. There, the opioid epidemic is so devastating that the foster care system has been overwhelmed by children who have become the detritus of addicted parents.

Experts on substance use disorders who have tracked the etiology of opioid addiction would also see a familiar theme with respect to how Irish went from being a supervisor at a fabrication company to the perpetrator of a drug store robbery.

After suffering a back injury in 2006, he was prescribed OxyContin during a period when pharmaceutical companies where downplaying its addictive properties, financial incentives led doctors to over-prescribe opioid pain medications. Naïve authorities failed to perceive the signs of misuse and abuse going on around them because addicts did not fit the stereotypical image of "dope fiends."

They resided in the heartland.

They worked and went to church on Sundays.

They weren't dark-skinned and had no accent.

During the 12 years that have elapsed since Irish was confined, legions of young men and women went from pilfering their parents' pills when they were teenagers and snorting them with friends to shooting heroin. Nurses have lost their jobs for stealing narcotics from their elderly patients. Countless men and women have lost custody of their children.

Let us pause for a moment to reflect on the crack epidemic, the policies it generated, and the character attacks on the addicts. Whether America learned from these mistakes, specifically whether the socio-demographic and white complexion of many contemporary opioid addicts brought enlightenment with respect to this latest drug epidemic, I can only guess.

In any case, the criminal justice system is already bursting at the seams due to mass incarceration. It therefore comes as no surprise to me that officials have lost the appetite to use demonization and imprisonment as expedients for dealing with the opioid epidemic— especially since the problem exists within their own communities.

I can imagine policymakers deliberating about establishing drug courts, implementing diversion programs, and funding more treatment centers now that a drug epidemic is not confined to the inner city.

"These people need help. They have a disease. We can't just lock them up and throw away the key," I can hear them saying.

Left Out

But those still confined before these sentiments affected the criminal justice system are seemingly left out of such discussions.

Recall that retribution was warranted because it was believed that these people were driven solely by their criminogenic needs. Their addictions, in and of itself, manifested they had little interest in being a part of law-abiding society.

But that was the past. The scientific consensus that opioid addiction is a disease undermines the deterrent and retributive purposes of punishment in these cases, leaving only incapacitation for rehabilitation.

Regardless, those confined before this paradigm shift have got nothing coming. Far too many of them present unsympathetic images due to their current convictions and dark skin complexions.

But make no mistake about it: If 10,000 soccer moms were languishing in prison for pulling capers to obtain prescription pain medication, lawyers would be battling to get them executive clemency or, alternatively, judicial relief based on arguments that these new socio-medical findings satisfy the legal standard for newly discovered evidence and warrant resentencing hearings to present mitigating factors in support of reducing their prison sentences.

That said, it remains a mystery how many years will pass before policymakers provide relief to those locked away in penitentiaries because their *disease* drove them to commit crimes to secure more— and more—prescription pain medication.

Until then, Corey Irish will continue serving out a sentence that exceeds the minimum term that is imposed on those who commit premeditated murder.

—*Feb.* 7, 2019

15

THE DANGEROUS (AND DELUSIONARY) 'BIG HOUSE SYNDROME'

Inmates sometimes believe that striking up friendly relationships with corrections officers is a useful strategy. Jeremiah calls it a prison-based version of the Stockholm Syndrome—and argues that it can be just as manipulative.

Almost a decade ago, Bruce Ramsey, a 47-year-old lieutenant at Washington State Reformatory (WSR), died in a tragic motorcycle accident. He had been a longtime member of the WSR staff, and his professionalism, along with his personality, not only garnered him the respect of his colleagues—but also, uniquely, the respect of many prisoners at the facility.

I cannot attest that his reputation was justified, since I had not been at the facility very long and had no interactions with him before he died.

However, several of my acquaintances who weren't prone to hyperbole spoke of their affinity for the lieutenant and assured me his reputation was well earned. They wished that the other officers at the facility would try and emulate him.

I understood their sentiments. I know several correctional officers and staff who execute their duties in a way that has earned my respect, too.

That said, when I saw the flyer notifying inmates that a memorial service for the lieutenant was going to occur inside WSR's chapel, I was perplexed. A few weeks later, when I was heading to the law library and saw the long line of prisoners patiently waiting to get inside of the chapel for the memorial service, I was taken aback.

When I later learned that a prisoner in attendance (who is a sexual psychopath and compulsive liar) cried on stage, and with quivering lips told the dead man's family that the lieutenant was his "friend"—I was absolutely disgusted.

For years thereafter, I could not get to the bottom of why this entire episode troubled me so much. Older and wiser, I can now explain the strange phenomenon that was writ large that day inside the prison chapel which caused my negative feelings to boil over.

The "Friend" Delusion

Inside a penitentiary, there's something called "the Big House Syndrome," which bears a resemblance to the Stockholm Syndrome, in which hostages develop a psychological alliance with their captors.

It is most prevalent inside Medium and Minimum Custody facilities, especially those that are not overly repressive.

The longer prisoners are confined within them, the more susceptible they are.

The symptoms are manifested in more mundane ways than prisoners attending memorial services for those who in life were paid to kill them to prevent their escape attempts from succeeding. For instance, I often see the same prisoners laughing and socializing with the same officers throughout their shifts five days a week, as if they are best friends or close colleagues.

To a convict, these interactions are justified only if the prisoner is endeavoring to prevent being targeted, to corrupt or compromise, or to cloak the prisoner's illicit activities. However, those with Big

House Syndrome actually believe these staff members are their friends, ignoring that the duties of correctional employees make befriending prisoners and maintaining professionalism mutually exclusive.

How could an officer be the friend of someone that he might have to gun down from the watch tower to stop a fight or riot?

How could she countenance confiscating items she believes do not threaten security from a "friend" who holds them dearly?

They can't—and they shouldn't try to convince themselves or pretend otherwise. The orderly operation of correctional facilities is enhanced, I believe, when custody staff remain aloof from prisoners, restricting most interactions to those which are necessary to perform their duties.

An occasional joke or friendly exchange is one thing. But overall, it is best practice for correctional officers to not entertain endless small talk from prisoners, especially those with Big House Syndrome. Feel free to move them along when they try to stop and preen.

Knowing Your Place

I don't recall such chitchat and other foolishness during my 15-year span confined in Level Four (Closed Custody) prisons, which are one custody level above solitary confinement. In that highly secure and dangerous environment, everyone knew their place, and almost everyone stayed in it to ensure their well-being.

Staff members who were impudent enough to buck the separate-and-unequal system of social relations with prisoners were slandered and ostracized by colleagues, especially in the case of apparent fraternizing between female staff members and prisoners who seemed too familiar.

Prisoners who refused to stay out of correctional officers' faces would be warned by other convicts to desist. If they persisted, they would get pummeled and stomped by associates, run out of general population by threat of further violence, and then have to spend the remainder of their sentences in protective custody.

Being polite and respectful was accepted, mainly because being rude or disrespectful could unleash aggressive reactions from prisoners and correctional officers alike. But as a rule, keeper and kept did not distort the truce nature of the relationship, no matter how friendly or sociable the other presented themselves to be.

To suggest that a friendship existed between a correctional officer and prisoner was actually offensive, because it implied one was compromised and would violate his duties for the prisoner's sake, and the other had bonded with the officer to such an extent that he is prone to snitch.

Quite simply, the prevailing prison norms require that each maintain a cool distance.

Otherwise, the maltreatment of prisoners would be difficult for many officers to countenance, and they might be unwilling to validate the lies in a colleague's incident report narrating how some prisoner supposedly committed a disciplinary violation. Likewise, prisoners might refuse to stand aside when an officer was being assaulted and could feel compelled to rescue their "friend" in distress.

The only way that both parties can, with equanimity, witness cruelty and be cruel when necessary is to harden their hearts.

Being forged in this way essentially immunized me against Big House Syndrome.

The Flim-Flam Men

While the Big House Syndrome ensured that plenty of prisoners would attend a memorial service for a correctional officer, the real executive producers behind the production are prison administrators for whom this approach satisfies their own interests.

WSR is unique in that officials at this facility have a long history of holding regular meetings with elected prisoner representatives, as if the conditions of confinement come by way of a collaborative process.

Both parties are motivated by self-interest: Make no mistake about it.

Administrators create the fiction that they are open and responsive to the concerns of prisoners. Meanwhile, the prisoner representatives often play along to curry favor and maintain the ability to have personal issues addressed due to their proximity to those in authority.

Why these prisoners are motivated to collaborate is often the result of their sentence structures rather than Big House Syndrome.

They are lifers.

They want to be freed.

This will only occur through executive clemency.

Consequently, by shucking-and-jiving, these prisoners hope to craft a narrative that will someday convince the Governor that their rehabilitation is extraordinary, and they are worthy of being set free.

I am convinced that an elected representative with a similar cast of mind suggested pitching the idea of having the memorial service for the lieutenant to administrators, and the rest of the representatives jumped on board to further their own interests. Then, once they got the go-ahead, they set about trying to persuade as many prisoners as they could to come and attend.

Reflecting on the statements that were made prior to the event led me to draw this conclusion.

"If the officers see how we're willing to honor one of theirs who was decent, maybe they'll see the value in acting more like he did," I heard one explain to a group of naive youngsters under his sway.

"If we convince these fools that we really care about this bullshit, maybe the administration will loosen up and let us have more shit," another candidly explained to me, believing I was so jaded that his logic would appeal to me.

Cynicism, peer pressure and self-interest ultimately led to a pretense of humanity. But I truly wish that administrators and prisoners would have never troubled that deceased man's family.

No matter how the service came into being and the pews were filled with prisoners, Big House Syndrome is the only sensible explanation for what caused the quivering lips of the rapist to tearfully bawl out from the stage that the lieutenant was his "friend."

The Model Prisoner's Demise

My friend is dying from a blood disease.

He has long been a prisoner at WSR, and his model behavior and personality not only earn him the respect of his peers but also, uniquely, from many officers at the facility.

But when he dies there will be no flyers inviting prisoners to attend a memorial service in his honor. Correctional officers will not be lined up to get inside of the prison chapel to pay their respects. Life will simply move on as it did the day before.

This captures why I never entertained the idea of entering the prison chapel all those years ago to honor that respected lieutenant. Life simply moved on for me as it did the day before, protected by a hard heart and enduring the life sentence imposed upon me when I was 14 years old.

—*Aug. 2, 2019*

16

FEAR, LOATHING, AND PRISON ROMANCES

Ordinary disciplinary measures for violating prison policy apparently aren't enough when an inmate develops a relationship with a staff member or volunteer.

Throughout my 27 years of confinement in the Washington Department of Corrections (WDOC), I have seen scores of women—from staff members to volunteers—barred from facilities or escorted off the premises after their prison romances were uncovered by internal investigators.

If maintaining security was paramount, these women would be encouraged to promptly vacate their positions once "compromised," in the vernacular of WDOC, and begin visiting like other members of the public in a room that is under proper surveillance.

This would be the most effective means to address the security threat posed by these relationships.

However, the ugly truth is prison officials cannot stomach these women's perceived "bewitchment" by convicts.

For allowing a convict to turn into a friend or fiancé, ordinary disciplinary measures for violating prison policy aren't enough.

These women must feel the full weight of the system's retribution, deterrence, disgust, and animus.

The roots of this attitude are much deeper than prejudice towards the incarcerated. There is a deeply racist dimension similar to that which exploded following the U.S. Supreme Court's 1954 decision in *Brown v. Board of Education*, which called for the integration of the public education system.

Segregationist opponents of integration worried that enabling impressionable children of different races to intermix would lead white children to see the humanity in (or find commonality with) their colored classmates—thereby undermining the historical meme that black people had "no rights which the white man was bound to respect," as the Supreme Court stated a century before in the *Dred Scott* decision.

In interracial schools, white girls might eventually get it into their heads to date black boys, and vice versa, the argument went. Their "fears" were realized. Census data confirms the rise in interracial marriages since the *Brown* decision—more particularly since the Supreme Court's 1967 *Loving v. Virginia*[1] ruling outlawed state statutes banning miscegenation.

By 2015, 17 percent of all new marriages in the U.S. were between spouses of a different race or ethnicity.[2]

The lesson is this: When opposite sexes have regular contact, romantic feelings can arise, even when the attraction is towards someone who is stigmatized, and an intimate relationship is taboo. Proximity is all that is necessary to overcome innumerable sessions of brainwashing that was intended to prevent women from falling into the hands of the wrong type of men.

This insight illustrates why unauthorized romances haunt the imaginings of prison officials who are tasked with maintaining security.

Safety and Security: Behind the Rhetoric

Security dangers aside, prisoners (regardless of their skin complexions) are akin to the African-American boys whom racists believed were just itching to caress their daughters' milky white skin. Like school integration and interracial marriages, the act of loving someone who has been legally and rhetorically framed as "other" begins to erode the distinction between "us" and "them."

Hence, correctional administrators are willing to do anything to prevent the white female staff and volunteers from getting into the clutches of convicts.

It begins during training.

As with blacks during the era of segregation, prisoners are maligned by a narrative designed to ensure that these women toe the line.

Prisoners are master manipulators, so it goes. Every interaction is part of a stratagem to get authorities to do their bidding. Impressionable staff are warned that inmates spend countless hours plotting to gain the trust of female staff and volunteers—one seemingly benign request and innocent verbal exchange at a time.

So, it is incumbent upon her to never divulge any personal information because prisoners will use it for some devilish purpose.

For instance, revealing the fact that she is a mother could lead to a conversation about parenting and cause her to perceive the prisoner as a father who loves his children rather than simply a convicted felon who lost his liberty. Then, a slippery slope that began with talk about the kiddies can result in a budding romance and the introduction of contraband—just as the slick convict intended.

At one Washington prison, the volunteer trainings take place in building that is also home to a wall-sized display case of prisoner-made shanks. The case is hung right outside of the bathrooms and ostensibly serves as a visual reminder to newly minted volunteers of the true insidious nature of the incarcerated men they will be interacting with.

Whether the rhetorical devices used in furtherance of this effort are hyperbolic, the putative purpose for this training is to reduce the likelihood that contraband will be smuggled in and out of the facility by lovelorn women with security clearances and prevent them from engaging in a host of other illicit activities for and at the behest of prisoners.

Yet despite the rhetoric, proximity wins out time and again.

Strangely enough, the very policies implemented by correctional systems undermine internal security because they often lead the "compromised" women to continue their clandestine relationships rather than come clean.

WDOC prohibits former staff members and volunteers from visiting a prisoner for three years.

This is surprisingly harsh for a "liberal" state. The wait period is well over three times the national average for former volunteers. Indeed, 74 percent of all states have a wait period of one year or less. Of those states, 71 percent impose no wait time at all.

Given that the WDOC waiting period is the average length of most prison sentences, it comes as no surprise to me that so many women decide to go underground once smitten. Far better to enjoy the company of a secret beau than spend three years without them.

Instead of strengthening security, such policies end up weakening it. Prison officials appear to be willfully blind to the reality that delayed gratification has little appeal to a person who has the option to use stealth to remain close to someone that they care about. Yet each passing day provides another opportunity for the nightmare scenarios feared by correctional administrators to play out.

The drugs.

The cellphones.

The sex.

The escapes.

Ironically, the Machiavellian prisoners that these women were forewarned about in training are the actual beneficiaries of such policies.

They rejoice in outcomes that ensure a female staff member or volunteer will decide to cloak her romance with a prisoner—who is running game unbeknownst to her—instead of quitting. The last thing these schemers want is for her to be under the watchful eyes of the guards inside of the visiting room.

Words of Wisdom

Allyson West, Executive Director for the Volunteer Reentry Program at San Quentin, has sage advice[3] for volunteers who decide to pursue relationships with prisoners:

If you fall in love, whatever kind of love that is—platonic, romantic, whatever, but most commonly romantic love—all you have to do, once you realize you want to cross that line, is quit the program. Take a month off, get on his visiting list, and go have a great relationship.... in my 18 years here, I've never met one (inmate) that wasn't worthy of our love. So if you fall in love, you go fall in love, I will dance at your wedding. I will give you away if you quit the program and protect the program and protect yourself and protect him.

Go live happily ever after and I will give you every blessing. So that's the right way. Because people are people, and you put people together, there are going to be some attractions that happen sometimes. And if you want to act on it, then you just have to do it appropriately.

As for volunteers in Washington State prisons, they will undoubtedly continue to use stealth and secrecy due to WDOC policy.

—Aug. 15, 2019

17

LEAVING 'PRISONEYLAND': A (NOT SO FOND) FAREWELL TO PRISON LIFE

On October 28, 2019, Jeremiah was released after serving 27-1/2 years of his life sentence. But even as he prepared for release, Jeremiah reports that he found it hard to let go of the "trauma induced by incarceration." This was the last column for TCR that Jeremiah wrote from confinement.

Science teaches that evolution is a slow process. Evolution instructs that a species that cannot adapt to its environment will go the way of the Neanderthal.

The Washington Department of Corrections is slowly evolving, too. It remains to be seen how many prisoners and staff go extinct in the process of bringing more humanity to WDOC facilities.

When I entered prison in 1993, convicts began teaching me how to survive in the midst of inhumanity. WDOC also shaped me by means of compulsion and solitary confinement. When I was physically resistant or noncompliant, brute force was employed by staff.

Eventually, special deterrence kept me in line—most of the time.

Once I became outwardly pacified, my counselors described me to their superiors at my annual reviews as an "easy keeper," which is a complement that means I rarely if ever bothered them for anything. Correctional officers also began nodding at me politely when I passed them by, because they saw that I minded my own business, was obedient, and was not rude or obnoxious.

In time, I received a custody "promotion" and was transferred to a hybrid Medium/Minimum Custody facility where I saw a new species of prisoner evolve that is far different than me.

For instance, when these new-breed prisoners are given direct orders by correctional officers they whine and ask "why?" as if they're owed an explanation. When I see them ask questions in the face of direct orders, I want to tell them, "Obey or disobey, just get to it."

These prisoners run to their counselors to ask questions rather than to just try to figure the answers out for themselves. When I hear them jabbering to their counselors about programs and good-time credit, I often think, "Leave these damn people alone. You're just going to annoy them, or they're going to talk down to you and make you regret coming to them for assistance."

These prisoners readily interact with officers, as if they are "homies" or former classmates. When I see them having frequent, lengthy conversations with officers I suspect the prisoner is either working an angle or has a propensity to snitch.

This is how my mind works: Although I no longer identify myself as a convict, I share many of the same sentiments because experience has demonstrated the logic behind the convict perspective.

Frankly, I feel more comfortable living in an environment where everybody knows their place—like on a Mississippi plantation before the Emancipation Proclamation.

Is this a sign that I am institutionalized?

Probably.

Yet I have plenty of company who wear uniforms and badges rather than prison khakis.

There are scores of correctional officers who share similar views due to their decades of working inside prisons, especially if they spent years employed in Closed Custody facilities—which are one level above solitary confinement and, as a rule, are rife with disciplinary misconduct and acts of violence fueled by drug addiction, greed, and plain old ignorance.

"Prisoneyland"

Their disdain for progressive policies and practices—and the new species of prisoners and staff—is captured when these officers use the term "Prisoneyland" to describe a place like Washington State Reformatory (WSR), where counselors exist who actually want to give "counsel" to the prisoners on their caseloads rather than simply be case managers who avoid direct contact.

These old-school officers seem just as bemused as me when they witness their new-school colleagues taking the time to explain the reasons behind the orders that they are giving to prisoners.

These new breeds also perceive me quite differently than staff members from the old school. My reticence and stoicism are often disconcerting, even though I politely nod my head in passing, mind my own business, and am not rude or obnoxious.

At best, I seem distant or standoffish. At worst, they think I have an attitude problem or am potentially dangerous.

Leaving my counselor alone to manage his or her caseload—as I make official public record requests to obtain and verify information told to me because past counselors have made me question their goodwill and integrity—does not make me an "easy keeper."

Instead, I seem arrogant and potentially malicious.

This is WDOC in the midst of an evolutionary process.

In the end, I doubt that I will ever have a less-jaundiced view of the new species of prisoners. As for my views on the ever-evolving staff members, things appear to be more promising.

A recent incident at WSR provides a perfect illustration.

One afternoon, I stood in the gymnasium for 15 minutes, waiting to get some water, watching the following scene unfold in front of the drinking fountain.

A female officer was calmly talking to a prisoner who was obviously upset. A male officer stood off at a distance, close enough to assist his colleague if necessary, but far enough away to not escalate the situation by seeming to be a hostile presence to the prisoner.

I have no idea what was said. But finally, the prisoner was sent back to his unit and I got my water, and as I returned to the gym, I heard the female officer tell someone on the phone that the prisoner had been "agitated" for several days, so unit staff should be cautious around him.

Note that segregation is where prisoners usually go when staff must be "cautious" around them, because any such prisoner arguably threatens the orderly operation of WDOC facilities and solitary confinement provides a remedy that can guarantee everyone's safety.

Treated as a "Human Being"

Yet this officer talked to the prisoner as if he were a human being rather than just a convicted felon, who is here to obey and be punished. Then she just sent him back to his unit, and he suffered no repercussions.

It was astonishing.

As I had become frustrated at my inability to gain access to the water fountain, I thought, "Why don't they just handcuff his ass and get this bullshit over with."

I couldn't help it.

It is hard to let go of the trauma that was induced by years of imprisonment in facilities where I was treated like an object. There are too many reminders. The ugly truth is that this treatment can occur on any given day inside any correctional facility, even Prisoneyland, and it reinforces the negative sentiments I developed from dealing with staff who act arbitrarily, capriciously, and with unnecessary hostility.

It is two steps forward and one step backwards in WDOC's mission to become more progressive.

For instance, not long after I witnessed the above incident and felt I had gained enlightenment, a different female officer became aggressive toward me because I stopped to ask the recreation officer a question in the middle of her conversation with him.

I was polite and said, "Excuse me," but no matter; she glared, then made a veiled threat to have me thrown in segregation for purportedly being Out of Bounds, which is a disciplinary violation for being in a restricted area.

I truly regretted my lapse in judgment. In the end, I brought it on myself by thinking I could approach them and be treated with civility.

Her antics reinforced my antiquated views as to why it is best to have as little to do with these people as possible. It is the safest course of action when people like this have the power to destroy you.

It is therefore no surprise why being confined from the age of 14 to 42 has made normal, humane interactions with staff often feel unnatural to me. This is how I have survived amongst predators with badges: I adapted to this dangerous habitat by adopting the ways of a convict.

Fortunately, I've been granted parole so I can finally go extinct.

—*Oct. 28, 2019*

CODA

BACK IN THE WORLD AGAIN

A month after his release, Jeremiah took stock of his life. He soon learned what many other returning citizens have discovered: The end of a long incarceration is only the beginning of an often-traumatic transition to civilian life, even with supporting family and friends.

Once upon a time, the Washington Department of Corrections and the Indeterminate Sentence Review Board (ISRB)—which has jurisdiction over a small subset of prisoners serving indeterminate sentences—had a joint policy whereby prisoners who have spent over 20 years confined for crimes they committed as minors were required to transition into the community in order to be freed.

Upon being found releasable, these prisoners had to agree to spend an additional year or more confined, beyond their minimum terms, moving through lower levels of custody—from Medium Security to Minimum Security to Camp to, finally, partial confinement for six months at a Work Release facility.

Through this entire time, they had to remain disciplinary-infraction free, following the dictates of correctional administrators with respect to reentry programming.

The policy governing this transition period is referred to as a Mutual Reentry Plan. It is better known as the Mutual Agreement Plan, or MAP, which originated in Wisconsin's Department of Corrections in the 1970s.

Whatever the name or where it came from, the idea that prisoners who were confined as minors needed to ease back into society was offensive to me. Nobody slowly transitioned me to prison. I was thrown unceremoniously into an adult facility when I was a child, and prison officials were not bothered in the least.

As for release preparation, the statute that served as the putative basis for implementing this policy required that the DOC provide the programs and services necessary to prepare us for release—no later than five years prior to the expiration of the minimum sentence.

So, there seemed to be no legitimate bases to transition prisoners after they had already experienced five years of release preparation.

When I learned that I might have to transition after being found releasable by the ISRB I was aghast, quite frankly. Aside from the extra time that I would have to spend confined, I was convinced that the clauses contained in the MAP were little more than claw-back provisions empowering the ISRB to rescind a favorable parole decision—especially the proscription against receiving any disciplinary violation.

I had good reason to be wary.

When it comes to prison discipline, the US Supreme Court has made clear that "any evidence" is constitutionally sufficient to support a guilty finding.[1] Therefore, were I to transition in accordance with a MAP, "any officer" could derail my release simply by lodging a disciplinary violation against me because innocence—in this world—is not synonymous with not guilty.

Furthermore, any fool who was imprisoned with me might feel emboldened to try something stupid since I would be deterred from delivering a situationally appropriate response. Chastising can readily be perceived as threatening behavior and could lead the ISRB to reverse course and decide to keep me confined.

Through a prisoner's eyes, it is easy to see why the MAP is a dangerous thing.

Had the ISRB ordered my release in 2017 when I finished serving my 25-year minimum term, I probably would have gone along with a MAP out of jubilation and wariness. But an unfavorable decision led to outrage and incautiousness.

To channel my anger and focus my mind I made it my mission to destroy this policy.

The *Ohio State Journal of Criminal Law* was the forum in which I weaponized my pen by arguing that the MAP was leading to the unlawful confinement of prisoners who were similarly situated to me.

A year later, the Washington State Court of Appeals adopted my legal analysis and the MAP policy was invalidated.[2]

The judge who sentenced me to life without parole when I was 14 years old wrote to congratulate me, saying, "You are already proving your future value to society. The Court of Appeals benefited significantly from your analysis."

Months later, I was found releasable by the ISRB.

Confined since the age of 14—and now age 42—I would go straight to the streets in 60 days when my release address was approved. Had an observer who could read minds observed me during the period prior to my release she would have found my thoughts and actions curious, or alarming, depending on her understanding of the effects of stress, anxiety, and trauma.

My chest would get tight. My face would get tense.

Alone in the cell at night, I furiously dug in my nose, sometimes until it bled, obsessing over taking the Law School Admission Test.

I was plagued by involuntary muscle twitches as I worried about employment.

I experienced vertigo as I lay in bed trying to sleep.

It is noteworthy that I had a supportive family and loving fiancée waiting for me, money to get on my feet, marketable legal and writing skills, and a college degree. Nevertheless, I was still sleeping too much and disassociating.

I can only imagine what those who lack outside support or marketable skills will be experiencing during this 60-day waiting period—as they face being released after spending their teens, 20s, and 30s in penitentiaries.

One of the purposes of the MAP was to gradually reduce supervision and control over prisoners' environment and expose them to increased stressors so they can learn appropriate skills and behaviors to utilize once freed. The last thing officials want is for a prisoner—who has possibly been secretly anesthetizing the traumatic effects of long-term confinement—to snatch up a dope bag of bottles of booze when life on the outside becomes too difficult.

Mind-altering substances ingested by men with violent histories is a recipe for reoffending. Yet the nightmare scenario would be for one of us to grow frustrated, then angry, and then commit another violent offense.

I have felt these and other emotions since my release on October 28, 2019.

I grow frustrated doing simple things like packing bags for a weekend trip. I can suddenly cycle from crying silently on a bus—out of elation that I am free—to being consumed by rage when I think about prison.

In retrospect, I realize that there was more to the MAP than a claw-back provision for rescinding favorable parole decisions. Transitioning prisoners under these circumstances gave them time to get their minds right, save some money in partial confinement at work release facilities (where they do not have to worry about paying rent), and to deal with reentry (from navigating the demands of competing family members and friends to applying newfound skills) at a measured pace.

But any prisoner who agreed to spend extra time confined for those purposes is a fool, if you ask me. The mission of any prisoner with sense is to get free—the sooner the better.

There is a solution that could satisfy the competing interests between a prisoner's quest to obtain his liberty and enhancing public safety.

Prisoners who have been confined since they were teens could be found conditionally releasable a year or more before becoming eligible for release, then required to successfully transition to the community for the remainder of their minimum terms. This would address the ISRB and DOC's duty to "ensure the public safety."

It would also ensure that prisoners are not unlawfully confined because the transition would occur before they had a legal right to be freed—and thereby would not run afoul of the judicial decision that invalidated these agency's first attempt to institute a MAP for prisoners who are subject to the *Miller* fix.

It is a mystery why neither the ISRB nor DOC has lobbied to put this into practice.

Oh well.

I'm free.

We will now see if enduring 60 days of unremitting stress and anxiety while awaiting my release was enough time for me to hone the skills and behaviors to appropriately respond to the psychological pressure that is a natural component of reentry.

—Nov. 20, 2019

A LIFE IN PRISON

JEREMIAH BOURGEOIS INCARCERATION HISTORY, 1992-2019

May 1992: Confined at King County Youth Detention Center after being arrested at age 14.

October 1992: Transferred to solitary confinement at King County Jail after jurisdiction was waived by the juvenile court, allowing him to be tried as an adult.

April 1993: Convicted of Aggravated Murder in the First Degree and sentenced to life without the possibility of parole at age 15. Transferred to Washington Corrections Center, the Department of Corrections' intake facility in Shelton, Washington.

June 1993: Transferred to Green Hill School, a maximum-security juvenile detention facility. This transfer was made pursuant to an interagency agreement between the Department of Corrections and Department of Juvenile Rehabilitation.

October 1994: Transferred to Washington Corrections Center after turning 17 years old.

January 1995: Transferred to Clallam Bay Corrections Center, a high-security facility in the Olympic Peninsula. Bourgeois earned his GED shortly thereafter but began cycling in and out of segregation for short periods due to misconduct.

February 1996: Placed on administrative segregation at Clallam Bay Corrections Center after assaulting two correctional officers. For this, he spent 24 months in solitary confinement and received a consecutive three-month sentence after pleading guilty to two counts of custodial assault.

February 1998: Released back into general population at Clallam Bay Corrections Center.

April 1998: Placed on administrative segregation at Clallam Bay Corrections Center after assaulting a prisoner with a weight. For this, he spent nine months in solitary confinement.

January 1999: Released back into general population at Clallam Bay Corrections Center.

September 1999: Placed on administrative segregation at Clallam Bay Corrections Center after assaulting a correctional officer. For this, he spent 24 months in solitary confinement, and received a consecutive 13-month sentence for custodial assault.

September 2001: Released back into general population after being transferred to Washington State Penitentiary, a high-security facility in eastern Washington. This is the state's oldest and most violent correctional facility.

October 2005: Placed on administrative segregation at Washington State Penitentiary based on allegations that he compromised a staff member. During the four years that he was in general population at this facility, he earned his paralegal certificate and began studying the law independently.

July 2006: Released back into general population after being transferred to Washington State Reformatory, a medium-security facility in Monroe, Washington. Bourgeois began taking distance learning courses independently to earn his bachelor's degree.

July 2007: Placed on administrative segregation at Washington State Reformatory for fighting with another prisoner. Since shots were fired to gain his compliance when he ignored the tower officer's orders to cease, he spent nine months in solitary confinement.

April 2008: Released back into general population at Washington State Reformatory. He continued taking distance-learning courses and earned an Information Technology Certificate though a prison vocational program offered through Edmonds Community College. Later, he joined the prisoner advisory committee for the University Beyond Bars—a non-profit program that provides college to prisoners at this facility. Bourgeois also became a leader in the Concerned Lifers Organization.

July 2013: Placed on administrative segregation at Washington State Reformatory based on allegations that he posed a threat to security. After a three-month investigation the allegations were determined to be unfounded. While in segregation, his fiancée Aimee Muul helped him edit his first law journal article over the telephone.

October 2013: Released back into general population after being transferred to Stafford Creek Corrections Center, a medium and minimum-security facility in Aberdeen, Washington. His law journal article, The Irrelevance of Reform: Maturation in the Department of

Corrections, was published shortly thereafter. Bourgeois picked-up
on his distance learning courses and began to post blogs on the
Minutes Before Six site, which features writing by prisoners across
the country.

July 2014: Transferred to King County Regional Justice Center to be
resentenced in accordance with legislative changes made in response
to the U.S. Supreme Court's decision in Miller v. Alabama (2012).

July 2014: Transferred back to Stafford Creek Corrections Center.

February 2015: Transferred to Coyote Ridge Corrections Center to
participate in reentry programming. It was the very programming he
had critiqued in his 2013 law journal article, maintaining it is
"pseudo-rehabilitative."

November 2016: Transferred back to Stafford Creek Corrections
Center. Began working to develop a restorative justice program with
another offender, Matthew Leon. Also began working with his
fiancée and others to obtain public records related to negligence and
misconduct within the Department of Corrections. These records
and related materials were the genesis for his first article in The
Crime Report. As Bourgeois' parole hearing approached, he began
having psychosomatic- induced seizures believed to be caused by
stress and anxiety.

February 2018: Transferred to Washington State Reformatory to
participate in further programming after he was denied parole in
October 2017. While awaiting his next parole hearing, he continued
having seizures. He also earned his bachelor's degree, graduating
magna cum laude. Additionally, he published two more articles in
law journals, one of which was cited by the Washington Court of
Appeals. The Court quoted Bourgeois directly, adopting his analysis

of the law regarding the statutory mandate to release juvenile offenders who were sentenced to over twenty years of confinement.

October 2019: Released from Washington State Reformatory.

EDITOR'S NOTE

Nancy Bilyeau, deputy editor of *The Crime Report*, played a key role in coordinating the editorial, art and production of this book, and championing it. Ricardo Martinez, office manager of the Center on Media, Crime and Justice, helped manage the logistical and financial details; Laura Devries of John Jay's Marketing and Communications Department created the cover design; and Richard Relkin of John Jay Marketing & Communications assisted in promotion. Sue Trowbridge created the ebook itself.

Jeremiah wishes to thank his fiancée Aimée Muul, and his sister, Paul Bourgeois—two of the most important people in his life, without whose love and support these essays would never have been possible.

We would also like to offer a special thanks to Karol Mason, President of John Jay College, for her steadfast support of *The Crime Report*.

NOTES

1. Breaking Good: How to Heal a Life Spent Behind Bars

1. https://www.seattletimes.com/seattle-news/new-law-puts-killer-who-got-life-sentence-as-a-teen-on-path-to-parole/
2. http://everymondaymatters.org/
3. https://www.amazon.com/Every-Monday-Matters-Ways-Difference/dp/1404105123
4. http://restorativejustice.org/rj-library/restorative-justice-and-the-practice-of-imprisonment/8675/#sthash.jmo8ZHHC.dpbs
5. http://mereps.foresee.hu/en/segedoldalak/news/179/c6e8f2a418/281/
6. https://www.nij.gov/topics/corrections/recidivism/pages/welcome.aspx

2. 'I Don't Know If I Will Ever Be Able to Get Over This'

1. https://www.oyez.org/cases/2011/10-9646
2. https://www.seattletimes.com/seattle-news/a-killer-at-14-he-remembers-no-life-but-prison/
3. http://courts.mrsc.org/supreme/117wn2d/117wn2do175.htm
4. https://www.law.cornell.edu/supremecourt/text/442/1
5. https://www.law.cornell.edu/supremecourt/text/427/215
6. http://courts.mrsc.org/supreme/075wn2d/075wn2do768.htm
7. https://www.amazon.com/Rethinking-Risk-Assessment-MacArthur-Disorder/dp/0195138821
8. https://www.oyez.org/cases/2011/10-9646

3. 'Every Prisoner in America Should Be As Angry as Me'

1. "Inferno: An Anatomy of American Punishment"
2. https://kb.osu.edu/bitstream/handle/1811/85820/OSJCL_V15N2_451.pdf?sequence=1&isAllowed=y
3. https://docplayer.net/68283282-Unmitigated-punishment-adolescent-criminal-responsibility-and-lwop-sentences.html
4. https://www.amazon.com/Philosophy-Imprisoned-Love-Wisdom-Incarceration/dp/1498500714

5. http://minutesbeforesix.blogspot.com/search/label/Jeremiah%20Bourgeois%20%28WA%29

4. Pretense, Prison, and the Free World

1. https://www.prisonlegalnews.org/media/publications/bureau_of_justice_assistance_homelessness_and_prisoner_reentry.pdf
2. https://nyupress.org/books/9780814770627/
3. https://www.ncjrs.gov/txtfiles/fs-9421.txt
4. https://www.ncjrs.gov/App/Publications/abstract.aspx?ID=120866
5. https://www.ncbi.nlm.nih.gov/pubmed/8746147
6. https://www.ncbi.nlm.nih.gov/pubmed/3608666

5. The 'Extraordinary' Ordinary Prisoner

1. https://www.seattletimes.com/seattle-news/crime/washington-prison-reformers-debate-bringing-back-parole/
2. https://komonews.com/news/local/former-three-striker-released-by-inslee-back-in-jail-accused-of-string-of-robberies
3. https://www.kiro7.com/news/local/3-strikes-felon-sentenced-to-life-in-prison-is-released-early-now-charged-with-murder/651736443/
4. https://www.seattletimes.com/seattle-news/writers-world-life-behind-bars/
5. https://thecrimereport.org/2017/02/23/a-prisoners-dream-and-disillusionment/
6. https://www.seattleweekly.com/news/inside-the-battle-to-bring-parole-back-to-washington-state/

6. Why Isn't There a #MeToo for Imprisoned Women?

1. https://www.amazon.com/Invisible-Woman-Justice-WADSWORTH-CONTEMPORARY/dp/0495090557
2. https://justpublics365.commons.gc.cuny.edu/12/2013/formerly-incarcerated-women-abuse/

7. 'They're Not Monsters': The Roots of Young Girls' Violence

1. ttps://www.amazon.com/Girls-Violence-Criminal-Behavior-Qualitative/dp/1588268381

8. The Ordeal of Gay and Transgender Prisoners

1. https://www.amazon.com/Place-Justice-Story-Punishment-Redemption/dp/0307277305
2. https://www.amazon.com/Life-Without-Parole-Living-Prison/dp/1891487868
3. https://www.semanticscholar.org/paper/Social-confirmation-of-dysphoria-shared-and-privat-Strack-Coyne/4d0d8cd0f8aad91edabc4a07effd3ddb49820caa
4. http://www.mass.gov/eopss/docs/eops/publications/implementing-a-reentry-program-according-to-best-practices-march-2007.pdf
5. https://www.amazon.com/Knowing-People-Personal-Social-Psychology/dp/0073039969/ref=sr_1_1?ie=UTF8&qid=1502645524&sr=8-1&keywords=michael+lovaglia

9. Inside Prison, Racial Pride Often Looks Like Hypocrisy

1. https://books.google.com/books?id=gVIeAAAAQBAJ&pg=PA225&lpg=PA225&dq=Michael+Lovaglia+We+are+prejudiced+to+the+extent+we+feel+threatened+or+fearful&source=bl&ots=89azromhDq&sig=Yo3jnsOoanxtqj2vOAAa745BMUA&hl=en&sa=X&ved=oahUKEwiOxonx-5fcAhWGGTQIHZz1DHwQ6AEIKTAA#v=onepage&q&f=false

10. The Real Nightmare of Solitary

1. https://www.amazon.com/Zek-American-Prison-Arthur-Longworth/dp/0997029900/ref=sr_1_1?ie=UTF8&qid=1533092249&sr=8-1&keywords=Zek%3A+An+American+Prison+Story

11. Where Black Lives (Also) Don't Matter

1. https://www.amazon.com/Black-Image-White-Mind-Communication/dp/0226210766/ref=sr_1_1?ie=UTF8&qid=1535228828&sr=8-1&keywords=the+black+image+in+the+white+mind

12. Behind Bars, Rage Can Be Therapeutic

1. https://nij.ojp.gov/topics/articles/does-cognitive-behavioral-therapy-work-criminal-justice-new-analysis
2. https://www.amazon.com/Cage-Your-Rage-Inmates-Control/dp/0929310764
3. https://journals.sagepub.com/doi/full/10.1177/1462474517737048

13. The 'Womb-to-Prison Pipeline'

1. https://equaljusticesociety.org/2018/10/10/new-ejs-report-breaking-the-chains-2-the-preschool-to-prison-pipeline-epidemic/
2. http://www.blackprisonerscaucus.org/

14. America's Saddest Prisoners

1. https://law.justia.com/cases/washington/court-of-appeals-division-ii/2009/37591-5-09-doc.html

16. Fear, Loathing, and Prison Romances

1. https://supreme.justia.com/cases/federal/us/388/1/
2. https://www.npr.org/sections/codeswitch/2017/05/18/528939766/five-fold-increase-in-interracial-marriages-50-years-after-they-became-legal
3. https://www.earhustlesq.com/episodes/2018/11/8/the-big-no-no

Coda

1. https://supreme.justia.com/cases/federal/us/472/445/
2. https://law.justia.com/cases/washington/court-of-appeals-division-ii/2019/50055-8.html

WHO WE ARE

The Crime Report is published daily by the Center on Media, Crime and Justice at John Jay College, in collaboration with Criminal Justice Journalists. The nation's most comprehensive one-stop online source for news, research and commentary on criminal justice, its staff of award-winning journalists cover emerging justice issues in the U.S. and abroad. Endorsed by the American Library Association.

Learn more at www.thecrimereport.org.

Made in United States
Orlando, FL
22 November 2024

54306646R00075